11 X 11/01 (12/01)
25×5/07 ↙ 7/07

Celtic Knotwork

Cross slab at Hilton
of Cadboll, Easter Ross

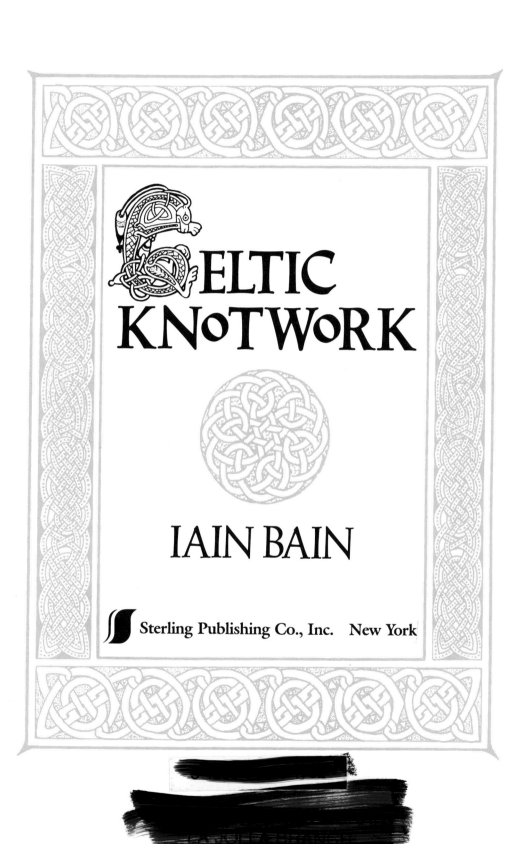

CELTIC KNOTWORK

IAIN BAIN

Sterling Publishing Co., Inc.   New York

Library of Congress Cataloging-in-Publication Data

Bain, Iain.
    Celtic knotwork / Iain Bain.
        p.   cm.
    Originally published: Constable, 1986.
    Includes index.
    ISBN 0-8069-8638-7
    1. Decoration and ornament, Celtic. 2. Repetitive patterns
(Decorative arts) I. Title.
NK1264.B35 1992
745.4′4941—dc20   91–39091
                                                CIP

10 9 8 7 6 5

First published in the United States in 1992
by Sterling Publishing Company, Inc.
387 Park Avenue South, New York, N.Y. 10016
Originally published in Great Britain by
Constable and Company Ltd © 1986 by Iain Bain
Distributed in Canada by Sterling Publishing
℅ Canadian Manda Group, P.O. Box 920, Station U
Toronto, Ontario, Canada M8Z 5P9
Manufactured in the United States of America
All rights reserved

Sterling ISBN 0-8069-8638-7

These worms are dedicated to Chirsty Ann

Cross slab No 2 at Aberlemno, Tayside

Contents

Illustrations

Acknowledgements

For setting me off on the right road by permitting me to consult the facsimile edition of *The Lindisfarne Gospels* with an introduction by E.G. Millar, British Museum (1923), my thanks go to the Literary and Philosophical Society of Newcastle upon Tyne, and particularly to Charles Parish, the Librarian.

For permitting me to consult the limited edition Urs Graf facsimiles of the *Book of Kells*, the *Book of Durrow* and the *Lindisfarne Gospels*, my thanks go to the Dean and Chapter of Durham, and particularly to Roger C. Norris, the Deputy Chapter Librarian, who also brought to my attention Miss Gwenda Adcock's Durham M. Phil. thesis, which is referred to in the Introduction of this book. Regrettably I have been unable to communicate with Miss Adcock, my several attempts to locate her whereabouts having so far been unsuccessful. I should be glad to hear from her if she reads this book.

For her kindness in answering my written questions (which I now realize span a number of years), my thanks go to Miss Janet M. Backhouse, Assistant Keeper, Department of Manuscripts in the British Library. One of these questions involved opening up the fragile *Lindisfarne Gospels*, and my thanks go to the Keeper also for agreeing to this rare action. The answer encouraged me to pursue the double interlacing construction which is described in Chapter 9.

For her help with the selection of photographs of sculptured stones for study, my thanks go to Dr Joanna Close-Brooks, of the then National Museum of Antiquities of Scotland. I am also grateful to that Museum, now part of the National Museums of Scotland, for permission to publish the black and white photographs of carved stones; to the British Library for permission to reproduce the colour pictures from the *Lindisfarne Gospels*; and to the Board of Trinity College, Dublin for permission to reproduce those from the *Book of Durrow* and the *Book of Kells*.

Having no expert to turn to, I value and am grateful to my daughter Sarah for studying and commenting on the manuscript as an ordinary reader. Lastly, my thanks go to Constable, in particular Prudence Fay, and to the designer Ivor Kamlish, for making order out of a chaos of typescript and sketches.

I.M.B. 1985

Preface

The art form which is the subject of this book has been steeped in mystery for some thousand years. The decorated knotwork produced by the ancients is comparatively easy to copy, but mere copying cannot unlock the mystery of its construction nor does it lead to creative use of the art. It is my hope that these methods for the reconstruction and creation of Celtic interlacing knotwork patterns will lead to an upsurge of interest in this fascinating subject.

In the sense that the methods cover a wide range of knotwork patterns from the very simple to the extremely complicated, they are not elementary; yet they *are* simple enough to be within the understanding of readers of almost any age and capability. Even those who may be put off by some of the simple mathematical symbols need not despair because these can be ignored, the mind being applied only to the grid lines, the diagonals, the quarter-points and the freely connected curves.

Indeed, I believe that this is an art form for the person who feels 'I can't draw, and this is far too complicated for me.' On the contrary, the simple disciplines of the construction-methods may surprise that person into an awareness of his or her completely unsuspected artistic ability.

Iain Bain 1985

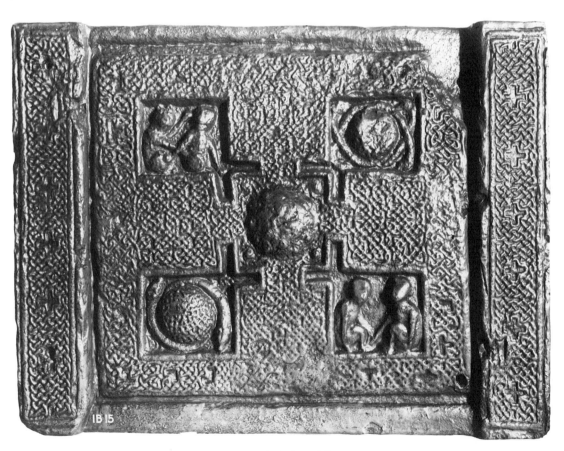

Sarcophagus at St Andrews, Fife

Introduction

In this age of rapidly increasing advancement in almost every field of science and technology, when it is difficult to keep up to date, either materially or mentally, there would seem to be a danger of older accomplishments being discarded and forgotten.

But this is not the case. More and more people are becoming interested and involved in the arts, crafts, customs and pursuits of the past, and obtain great satisfaction in doing so.

One manifestation of this leisure-time rebellion against today's automated living is a growing interest in the ancient art form of the Celts; an art form which was born in prehistoric times and died a thousand years ago. Enough examples of the art have survived, on carved stone, in jewellery, on metalwork and in the ancient illuminated manuscripts, for its greatness to be appreciated, but the absence of continuity and development in that art has meant that the original methods of its construction are obscure.

The beauty, complexity and excellence of design and workmanship achieved by the ancient Celtic artists and craftsmen can be seen in the examples of the originals reproduced in this book. All have a geometric appearance in the form of interlacing knotwork, or step patterns, or spirals, or key patterns, or interlacing human, bird, beast or reptile figures. As an art form it is unique, and the current popular interest which it inspires is a welcome and important phenomenon.

This interest, however, should not be confined to admiration of the original works. It should be concerned with the rebirth of the art not only in its original form but as a new expression of its Celtic origin. It is important, therefore, that the rebirth should be healthy so that it can develop to a new maturity.

There has been research into the methods of construction, and the pioneer of this would seem to have been the antiquarian J. Romilly Allen, FSA, whose painstaking work over many years is summarized in his *Celtic Art in Pagan and Christian Times*, published by Methuen & Co in 1904. This is a great work and it is difficult to understand why nearly half a century elapsed before the next stage of development, but there is more on this subject later.

The next stage was the work done by my late father, George Bain. His *Celtic Art. The Methods of Construction*, was published by William Maclellan in 1951, having first appeared a few years earlier in booklet form. In 1977 it was reissued in paperback by Constable. My father referred to the work as an elementary textbook prepared specially for use in elementary and secondary schools and to give instruction to art students, artists, and art workers in a multitude of crafts. The book was well received at home and overseas, and reprinted in hardback and softback many times; its popularity is a measure of the increasing interest in things Celtic. Until this book of mine, it was the only reference book on Celtic construction-methods available to artists and craftsmen.

An introduction to Romilly Allen's work had started my father on his quest, and as he progressed he became interested in the educational possibilities of the work he was doing. Between the wars I well remember his concern that Scotland's gift shops were full of tartan souvenirs, mainly shoddy and not even made in Scotland. He looked forward to the day when shops not only in Scotland but throughout Britain and overseas would display original works of Celtic art created and fashioned by artists from his teaching. Alas, that day has not yet arrived.

Recent years, though, have seen an upsurge in the whole range of traditional Scottish arts and crafts, in wood, pottery, glass, textiles, leather, copper, silver and other materials, and this has largely counteracted the 'tartan souvenir' image which my father deplored. There is, of course, a rightful place in Scotland for craft work based on the tartan theme, and much of this today is commendable. Encouragingly, some workers are using the Celtic theme, and here also good work is done, but unfortunately there are few examples of the real creative work my father hoped for. In the case of interlacing knotwork, most examples lack continuity and do not have the unique proportions which are such a regular feature of the ancient patterns. Particularly disappointing is the fact that most of the work consists merely of fragments copied from my father's book, or simple adaptations of these, thus defeating his main object which was that 'by understanding the method, new designs and even new methods in this peculiar art may be produced'.

In my youth I took no active interest in my artist father's diversion into the study of Celtic art. My future lay not in art but in engineering, and I had left home before he became seriously involved in the subject. Later on, when his booklets were published, I dabbled with his methods for the construction of interlacing knotwork, but I soon became confused and gave up trying to apply them.

Many years later, on a wet tour of northern Scotland, I visited a few craft workshops which contained examples of Celtic art. In each case *Celtic Art. The Methods of Construction* was the source of information and in some instances the craft-worker had known my father and discussed the work with him. It transpired that they too had difficulty in following my father's construction-methods for knotwork, firstly in controlling the final shapes and proportions and secondly in fitting a pattern into an available space.

These were exactly the difficulties I had found, but I had been able to dismiss the problem because I could put it down to my lack of training in arts and crafts. These craft-workers, however, were some of the very people his book was intended to help, and if it was not doing this then other methods of construction should be sought. After all, my father had stated that if the methods and their stages that were set out in his book were not those used by the ancients, then those could only prove to have been simpler – perhaps more ingenious but not more difficult. What if *no* specialized knowledge were necessary to discover and apply them? If that were a possibility, there was no reason why I should not tackle the problem myself. Thus began a spare-time task which became more compelling as it proceeded, each discovery leading to another question, in turn leading to another discovery and another question. Even today that pattern is continuing.

It must be emphasized, however, that my subject in this book is knotwork only, and no alternative construction-methods are offered here for the key patterns, spirals, zoomorphics and other forms of ornament contained in my father's book.

My first task was to analyse the difficulties which the craft-workers and I were having with my father's methods of knotwork construction. His methods did not give me the dimensional controls needed to guide my hand to the production of a finished pattern that looked remotely like the original. This did not surprise me, since I had always been awed by the remarkable facility he had with pen or brush. His hand was so sure that the methods he needed were not so much methods of actual construction as methods of guidance in maintaining the 'order' of the pattern, and he even used different methods to obtain the same patterns. This is illustrated in his book on pages 28 and 29, where three different centre-line methods produce the same pattern.

Method 1

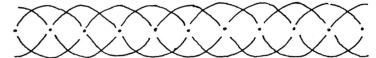

Commence with a row of dots, then arch over and under in two spaces.

Method 2

Use Shape A to commence the arching.

Method 3

Stagger the dots and arch one space over and two spaces under.

The pattern from the *Lindisfarne Gospels* folio 95 shown below is produced on his Plate B and Plate 2 by methods 1 and 3, and could equally well be produced by method 2. (There could also be a method 4 which would be method 3 turned upside-down.)

The proportions of the patterns he constructed by all three methods are acceptably close to the ancient originals. So also is the rendering above, which was produced by my methods that are the subject of this book (see Plate 2).

Clearly my father's mental preconception of the final pattern on the blank paper was such that he could place his guiding dots and arches very nearly, if not exactly, in their proper positions. There is no doubt that he himself had the quality which he credited to the ancient scribes of 'visualising beforehand a completed work in its final state and materials'. It is an ability that comparatively few people share.

Unfortunately in using my father's methods the overall width of the pattern is the last dimension to be established, because the pattern grows outwards from the dots, the extent depending on the shape of the curves and the chosen band (cord) thickness. In seeking a different approach, which would enable the overall dimensions of a pattern to be chosen first, I thought of the strong diagonals as possible setting-out lines, using the edge lines of the cords instead of their centre-lines. This was in keeping with my father's methods of key pattern and spiral construction, in which the setting-out lines form part of the final pattern.

This led me to the discovery of the 'approximate' geometry of the curved portions of the cords, and hence the ability to reconstruct a whole range of Celtic patterns, all of which had the unique proportions of their originals in the ancient works such as the *Lindisfarne Gospels*, the *Book of Kells* and the *Book of Durrow*, and on the monumental carvings.

Some problems yet remained to be solved, including the mystery of how the ancients preconceived the block setting-out for masterpieces like the full-page illuminations in the manuscripts. Then, in 1980, copies of J. Romilly Allen's works came into my possession. In 1904, in his *Celtic Art in Pagan and Christian Times* to which I have already referred, he stated that the problem took him twenty years to think out, so that the task was already absorbing him in 1890 when he was entrusted by the Society of Antiquaries of Scotland to survey the sculptured stones of Scotland. The results of his survey appeared in 1903 in parts 2 and 3 of a publication entitled *The Early Christian Monuments of Scotland*.

The title is an understatement. His survey included a remarkably detailed analysis of the geometric forms of Celtic decoration, in knotwork, key patterns, and spirals, and it was not confined to those appearing on early Christian monuments, or to Scotland. He classified hundreds of different patterns occurring in Scotland and elsewhere in Britain and Ireland and in the rest of Europe, on sculptured stones, on metalwork such as reliquaries, chalices and brooches, on ivory, and in illuminated manuscripts such as the *Lindisfarne Gospels*, the *Book of Durrow*, and the *Book of Kells*.

This classification became possible with his original discovery that Celtic knotwork was evolved from the plait. He stated that 'in Egyptian, Greek, and Roman decorative art the only kind of interlaced work is the plait, without any modification whatever; and the man who discovered how to devise new patterns from a simple plait by making what I termed "breaks" laid the foundation of all the wonderfully complicated and truly bewildering forms of interlaced ornament found in such a masterpiece of the art of illumination as the *Book of Kells* in Trinity College, Dublin.'

His writings do not seem to have had much impact on the art world. Maybe this was because his illustrations of the patterns (and there are over 1,500), are diagrams intended solely for the purpose of classification so as to avoid repetitive descriptions. Yet he was an accomplished draughtsman, and there is no doubt that he fully appreciated the beauty of the art. In his *Celtic Art in Pagan and Christian Times* he refers to 'the beauty and individuality of the ornamental designs ... due chiefly to the great taste with which the different elements are combined and the exquisite finish lavished upon them'.

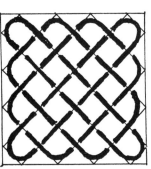

In studying *The Early Christian Monuments of Scotland* one could be forgiven for believing that he had failed to describe how he constructed his pattern diagrams, yet the construction is in fact so simple that it is contained in the introduction to his plait theory and in simple diagrams like the one alongside (above).

With the introduction of breaks, which he explains, this diagram actually enables all of his subsequent patterns to be drawn.

You will note that his diagram is of a continuous plait, and does not explain how the pattern could be terminated. It is interesting to compare this diagram with one a year later in *Celtic Art in Pagan and Christian Times* in which the plait is now contained within all four boundaries as shown below. In addition to solving end and

Cross at Lastingham,
North Yorkshire

11

corner treatment it goes a long way towards solving the problem of fitting the pattern into an available space.

Even more significant is his observation that 'the setting-out lines ought really to be double so as to define the width of the band comprising the plait, but they are drawn single on the diagram in order to simplify the explanation'.

Reduced to the simplest terms, the difference between the two diagrams is the difference between figures A and B below.

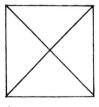 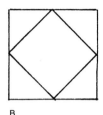 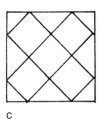

A   B   C

Convert figure B to figure C by doubling the diagonals so that they meet the sides at the sides' quarter-points, and a vista of design opens up. Whereas I had taken it for granted that the ancient artists and scribes had had almost superhuman mental vision when laying out the designs for a whole page of illuminations I now began to see that this was not necessarily so.

A common practice of the Celts was to combine two or more forms of decoration in the same overall design, but normally the different forms – knotwork, step patterns, key patterns, spirals and zoomorphic patterns – would be separated from one another in different panels of various shapes and sizes. Typical examples in the manuscripts are *Lindisfarne Gospels* folio 94b (Plate 1) and *Kells* folio 291V (Plate 3); and on the sculptured stones are Hilton of Cadboll and Aberlemno (frontispiece and page 2).

In the case of the knotwork (but I have no reason to suppose that it would not apply equally to the other forms of decoration), the panels could have been laid out regardless of the actual patterns finally to fill them, in the certain knowledge that the choice could be left until later, when they could either be freshly created or be selected from a library of patterns.

Sadly, familiarity, if it does not actually breed contempt, has a somewhat deflationary effect. No matter whether my methods of construction are those of the ancients or not, they make it easy to create or reconstruct knotwork patterns similar in proportion to the Celtic originals, in an infinite variety of enclosing shapes. In that aspect alone – that of construction, not of art work – it would seem that they did not need superhuman powers.

The thought which follows is that during their time they would not have been pleased for anyone to succeed in uncovering their secrets. Knowledge of the construction methods was fairly widespread, because examples of the same distinctive form of knotwork patterns can be traced from the Greek islands to northern Scotland, but it could hardly have been *common* knowledge.

The Christian Church was the patron of the arts during the heyday of the Celtic period. But in both pagan and Christian societies the only certain way of exerting power or commanding a following was by using fear; and there were two elemental fears – the fear of the sword and the fear of the occult. Indeed one wonders if human nature has changed much at all since Celtic times, because the word 'Godfearing' is still literally true in the northern and western extremities of the British Isles.

It is possible that the mystique of Celtic art, in both pagan and Christian times, would have been a closely guarded secret, giving to its practitioners similar powers to those of the magician, or medicine-man, or miracle-worker in the eyes of the beholder. In Christian times the illuminations were undoubtedly undertaken for the glorification of God, but the artist-priests would hardly have missed the chance to aid their cause with superstition.

But I do not intend to pursue the reasons for the existence of Celtic art. This is better left to those qualified to do so. These few thoughts have been included because it is impossible to spend any length of time studying the art without wondering why it originated.

To my knowledge there has been only one publication on Celtic knotwork construction-methods since my father's book, and this is not available to the general public. It is included in a two-volume Durham M.Phil. thesis written in 1974 by Miss Gwenda Adcock, entitled 'A Study of the Types of Interlace on Northumbrian Sculpture'.

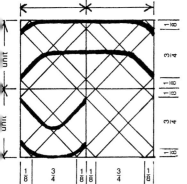

In its field her study is as comprehensive as Romilly Allen's. Her construction-methods are based on a squared grid, and like me she draws the edge lines of the cords rather than their centre-lines. She does not use diagonal setting-out lines, but draws the cords directly, establishing their positions from the points at which imaginary diagonals cross the grid lines, as shown left for a half-width cord.

Curved cords spanning two grid-units are like two halves of a curve spanning one grid joined together by a straight portion, and this is a disadvantage, especially when they are repeated through 360 degrees in what Romilly Allen termed circular knotwork. Miss Adcock goes further than either Romilly Allen or my father in that patterns produced by her methods ensure the proportions of the originals, apart from the boxiness of these 'long' curves.

She varies the position of the grid crossing-points to suit the width of the cords in each particular pattern, whereas I use the quarter-points of the grid sides for *all* standard pattern setting-out, and variation of cord thickness is merely one of many final renderings.

I would be surprised if any serious student of Celtic art did not at some stage become conscious that it expresses a kind of graphic language. Miss Adcock has certainly been able to translate some of this language, and it has enabled her to break new ground by reconstructing parts of the patterns on stones where they have been weathered beyond recognition. In the carvings the backgrounds are cut away, and the cords stand out in relief. Therefore when the cords are worn away, the areas between the criss-crossing cords remain as 'holes', and her knowledge of the language has enabled her to reconstruct the worn areas.

Another factor which must affect the construction-methods is the shape of the grid-unit, which establishes the slope of the diagonals. Miss Adcock uses the square, giving 45°. My father's knotwork borders do not have a fixed slope angle. His separate section of knotwork panels generally uses the square proportions, but he also uses what he terms the Pictish proportions of 1 by $\frac{3}{4}$, which in fact are the proportions of the anciently known 3:4:5 triangle, which gives a slope angle of approximately 37°. Romilly Allen's diagonals generally use the 45° slope angle, but he also depicts patterns in which the slope angle is, or very nearly is, in the ratio of 3:4.

Most original patterns clearly use the 45° angle, which conforms with construction on a square grid, and some seem to be derived from the 3:4:5 triangle, or very nearly so. But many patterns are constructed in panels which are not at all rectangular, so that a truly rectangular grid-unit is no aid to their construction. The panels can be circles or parts of circles, or triangles, or diamonds, or irregularly shaped with curving or tapering sides.

My observations have led me to believe that the minute detail of the manuscripts holds the key to the construction-methods. Careful measurements and ruled lines would be used in the setting-out, but all the finished line work would be applied freehand by quill and brush. Not only this would allow some freedom of expression. At the small scale, the thickness of the quill or brush strokes would significantly alter the cord thickness depending on whether they were applied straddling, or inside, or outside, the setting-out lines.

The same freedom of expression could also be used to fill irregularly shaped panels with knotwork designs, and sometimes even the setting-out could be drawn freehand.

The grid-unit with the diagonals drawn through the quarter-points is ideal for this purpose. The same pattern appears on both of the drawings shown below. The first shows all of the setting-out, which would normally be done in pencil. Both have been drawn freehand and although the patterns are similar none of the dimensions in one drawing is identical with those of the other.

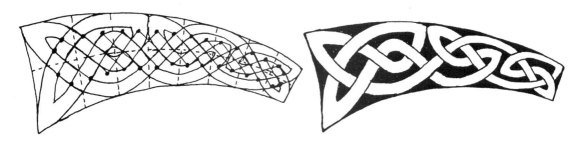

This freedom of line is one of the charms of Celtic art. It applies equally to illustrations in manuscripts and to the carved stones. Circles are rarely perfect. Cord thicknesses vary slightly, and even the angles of the diagonals vary slightly within the same pattern, as does the spacing of the diagonals. But it is likely to have been the freehand use of the stonemason's chisel and the scribe's quill and brush which caused the irregularities, for these irregularities would have been more pronounced had not the underlying setting-out been accurately drawn. It was the discipline of this underlying setting-out which gave Celtic knotwork the same form, proportions, and character throughout the Celtic world. Even with irregular panel shapes like those above, patterns with the same characteristics can be created once one has acquired the 'feel' of the art.

In submitting these construction-methods, I do not believe that that is the end of the matter. My hope is that they will stimulate the reconstruction and creation of Celtic works far more imaginative and ambitious than those appearing at present, and also encourage more research, because I am convinced that there are many discoveries still to be made.

Cross slab (side) at St Vigeans, Tayside

Cross slab (front) at St Vigeans, Tayside

For myself, I shall be satisfied if I can communicate some understanding of a lost art, so that those who wish to practise it will not unwittingly depart from its principles or change its character. There is nothing wrong with change so long as one knows what one is changing. Nowhere in Celtic interlacing will you find three cords crossing at one point, yet I have seen instances of this in Scotland in recent designs which undoubtedly were intended to be Celtic. One proffered reason was that it made a better detail, and another was that the design was the artist's own creation and was not intended to copy the Celtic form (although in all other respects it did so).

I can visualize two parallel paths which Celtic knotwork arts and crafts can follow, both using these construction-methods merely as tools to provide the setting-out information to aid the final art and craft work. On one path the final designs would be reconstructions or creations in the ancient classical form. On the other, modern treatments would evolve, bringing an entirely new dimension to the art.

The educational possibilities are considerable as my father proved in practice, and it is hoped that these new methods will be found simple to learn and to use. Undoubtedly, as with the computer, children will learn more quickly than adults, but because of the repetitive nature of the stages, some could find them boring.

The one certain fact is that there is an abundance of artists and craftsmen who admire and are fascinated by Celtic knotwork, and would use it in their work if they could. The construction-methods which follow will make this possible. Original Celtic patterns can be reconstructed or adapted, new patterns can be created, and all can be fitted into the shapes they are required to occupy. Some practice is needed to get used to the 'language', but thereafter the work becomes easy and rapid and satisfying.

My task will have been fulfilled if artists and craftsmen use these setting-out methods as aids to art work in conjunction with their own particular skills. To do that, however, craftsmen still have the problem of transferring the finished pattern from paper to the surface to be decorated, particularly for repetitive work, on materials such as leather, wood, metal, glass and pottery. Of this problem I have been constantly aware; but whichever methods they employ for transferring other decorations should be suitable also for Celtic knotwork.

Something else of which I have been constantly aware since I first noticed the approximate geometry of the curves, and later linked that with Romilly Allen's plait theory, is the apparent difference between those two theories and the evidence provided by prickings, rulings, and markings visible on the reverse side of some of the decorated pages in the *Lindisfarne Gospels*.

The possibility that the craft workers' problem in transferring patterns would explain that apparent difference did not strike me until this book was being processed for publication; but the explanation seems so simple and feasible that I then felt that its inclusion would be an important contribution.

Grid rulings on the reverse side of some *Lindisfarne* pages were referred to by E.G. Millar in *The Lindisfarne Gospels* published by the British Museum in 1923. This must have come to my father's notice. An excellent commentary on the prickings, rulings and other markings was made by R.L.S. Bruce-Mitford in the two-volume Urs Graf Verlag publication of the *Lindisfarne Gospels* in 1956 and 1960.

Facsimiles of these reverse-side markings are included along with the other facsimiles in Vol 1. In Vol 2, Bruce-Mitford illustrates and explains in detail the geometrical layout of the illuminated pages and the setting-out of much of the ornament. In the case of the knotwork panels, however, he surmises, rightly on the evidence, that after gridding the panel the pattern was drawn freehand, using imaginary crossing-points on the grid sides. It is this theory that Gwenda Adcock has pursued so admirably in her thesis 'A Study of the Types of Interlace on Northumbrian Sculpture'.

How can this be reconciled with Romilly Allen's or my father's plaits?

It can be, if the scribe's patterns were *copied* on to the vellum from a master drawing. First he would decide which pattern to use in a particular panel. This could be taken from stock of patterns, designed by himself or others, or else could be specially created. The chosen rendering would then be constructed on a suitable surface, possibly wax, in the required panel shape, but much larger than needed in the manuscript page, and the setting-out information would not be limited to grid lines. The manuscript would then be divided into the same number of grid-units, without additional setting-out lines which would only cause confusion on such a small scale. Finally, with the master-plan beside him, the scribe could draw the cords directly by watching the cord crossing-points on the grid lines. This fragment of circular knotwork is a rendering of the *Lindisfarne Gospels* folio 2b pattern at approximately the original scale, but the scribe Eadfrith also included a medial cord line (see the construction on page 72).

Such a method of transferring works of art from one surface to another has always been used, whether by Michelangelo for murals, by stage designers for backcloths, or more recently by painters using photographs to transfer information accurately on to canvas. My father designed and painted many stage settings, and I am sure he would never have associated Eadfrith's grid with a setting-out device. He would recognize it as a transfer guide.

My father would also have used a master-plan, which when completed would give him the margin by which its borders extended beyond his dots and chevrons (see page 9). Working to a larger scale than Eadfrith, he did not need a grid to transfer the pattern to its available panel. He would merely leave an equivalent margin within the edges of the panel and adjust the spacing of the dots and chevrons to fit the remaining space. He achieved remarkably accurate reproductions of the originals by this method, but even he tended to depart from the unique Celtic proportions when not concerned with reproduction.

Grid lines contribute little to the lines of the pattern, and even with my methods grid lines are unnecessary for rectilinear panels. They are, however, required for annular or irregular panels, because of the variable size of the individual grid-units, and they are worth drawing anyway because they aid the subdivision of the panel and the establishment of break points in the basic plait.

It is to be hoped that references to master craftsmen like my father and the genius Eadfrith do not discourage the ordinary reader for whom this book is intended. I have no doubt that ability similar to theirs, or to that of Michelangelo or Albrecht Dürer to name another two, exists today, but those who never hope to reach such standards may, like me, surprise themselves with what can be achieved by using these construction-methods.

18   Cross slab from Woodwray, Tayside

Seek a method of construction by observing a finished pattern. This repeating pattern is from the *Lindisfarne Gospels* folio 12.

It is their likeness to loosely knotted cords which has given the name knotwork to these peculiarly Celtic interlacing patterns.

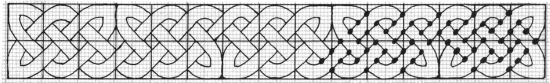

The pattern divides conveniently into a grid of squares, and if the interlace positions are spotted, a regularly spaced lattice is suggested.

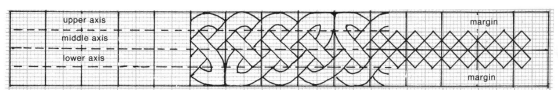

The cord crossings are on three axes. Each 'over' is followed by an 'under', and all the 'overs' on each axis face the same way.

The foundation of the pattern can be expressed as a grid containing a lattice surrounded by a margin.

Now develop the pattern from the start:

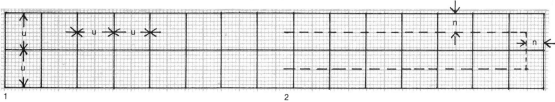

1 Draw the grid: u expresses its unit measurement.
2 Mark off a margin, width $n(\frac{u}{2})$ all around the pattern.

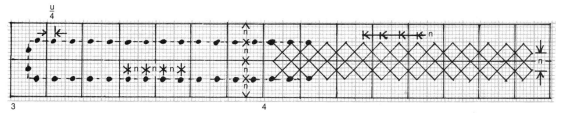

3 Spot the quarter-points, $\frac{u}{4}$ $(\frac{n}{2})$, all around the inside of the margin.
4 Draw the diagonals: n is the spacing of the diagonals measured parallel to the grid.

19

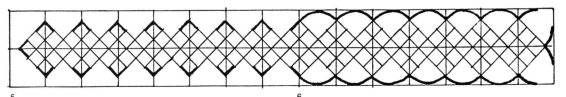

5 6

5 Extend those diagonals which will meet at the grid lines (they do so at the quarter-points).

6 Draw the outer curves of the cords, merging those at the ends into the border. Avoid kinks or reverse curves.

7 8

7 Draw the inner curves maintaining cord thickness. Complete the corners with short straight lines.

8 Erase lines to form a plait. The overlap order reverses from one axis to the next.

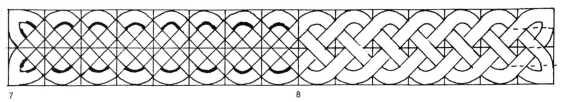

9

9 Erase the hatched portions of the plait.

10

10 Form the returns using the end treatment shown in stages 6 and 7. Again draw the outer curves first.

The work to stage 10 would normally be carried out in pencil and the whole would be the setting-out plan for the freehand creation of the finished design. In this instance the setting-out lines have been followed faithfully and the background has been darkened.

This pattern uses the 'short' curve. The next pattern also uses the 'long' curve. In patterns in which the short curve predominates, stages 4 and 5, or 5 and 6, may be combined with practice.

This pattern appears in the *Lindisfarne Gospels* on folio 94b and elsewhere.

The 94b (Plate 1) design is double-interlaced, as shown above. The cord lines are thickened and themselves become cords which are interlaced.

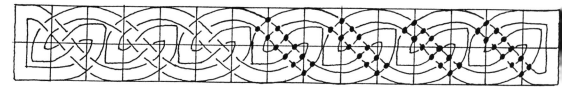

The double-interlacing does not affect the basic pattern. Again the pattern divides conveniently into a square grid, and when the interlace positions are spotted these suggest a regularly spaced lattice.

To develop the pattern, proceed as before to the stage 4 lattice foundation:

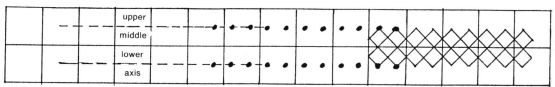

upper			
middle			
lower			
axis			

1 The grid.   2 The margins.   3 The quarter-points.   4 The lattice.

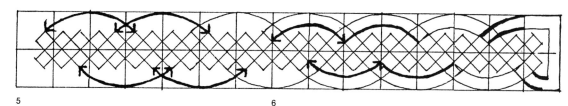

5   6

5 Draw the sweeping 'long' curves, the outer lines first, followed by the inner lines, maintaining constant cord thickness. The ↘s mark the springing points.
6 Draw the end treatment, straight lines leading round from half a long curve above to half a short curve below. The other end is upside-down.

7

8

7 Draw the cords around the middle axis with short curves and straight lines, outer lines first, the inner lines maintaining constant cord thickness. The inner short straights meet at a diagonal.

8 For a finished design with single-interlacing, erase the unwanted lines and fill in a dark background.

9

9 For double-interlacing, straddle each cord line with a double line. This flattens the curves somewhat, to keep them within the pattern space. Note that the overs and unders are the same at each double-crossing.

See also Chapter 9 for a special *Lindisfarne* double-interlacing construction.

Chapter 2

The Grid and its Cells

The Grid

Knotwork is only one of several forms of Celtic art decoration. Other forms are key patterns, step patterns, spirals and zoomorphics (intertwined birds, beasts, reptiles). Usually several of these forms appear on the same work of art, such as a monumental stone, a piece of jewellery, or metalwork, or in the illustrated manuscripts.

In studying the manuscripts, such as the *Lindisfarne Gospels*, or *Durrow* and *Kells*, one is filled with a sense of wonder at the knowledge and skills which enabled the ancient scribes to conceive and execute such beautiful and intricate designs. Even today the skills are beyond our understanding, particularly because of the minuteness of the detail, but the creation of the knotwork patterns, and their inclusion in panels of diverse shapes and sizes, is really very simple, once the 'language' is understood and the stage-by-stage build-up of the setting-out is mastered. Almost any panel shape can accommodate Celtic knotwork if it can be divided into a whole number of grid-units. The shape of the panel affects the shape of the grid-unit.

The commonest grid shape is the square, used in a square or other rectangular panel, or in the rectilinear parts of more complicated panel shapes. A good example is the layout for *Lindisfarne* folio 94b, shown on page 24. All of the forms of decoration referred to above appear in this full-page design. Knotwork is the main form, covering the whole page, but with areas cut out to make room for panels of the other forms. The circular portion is, however, evidence that not every grid-unit has to be a square, or even the same size.

Indeed, a common feature of the manuscripts is the decoration of capital letters with Celtic ornament. Here the panel shapes are irregular, and curved lines predominate, producing curved and tapered grid-units. But mostly the panels are rectangular, and if the grid-units are not square, their length exceeds their breadth but the ratio seldom exceeds 4:3. Irregularly shaped grid-units, which always have four sides, seem also to have been drawn with these proportions in mind.

Nearly all patterns may be drawn firstly on a square grid. (See page 80 for the standard version of the circular part of *Lindisfarne* folio 94b and also Plate 1.) The final choice will depend on personal preference and on the shape of the space the pattern is to occupy.

Fragments of cross slab from Tarbat, Easter Ross

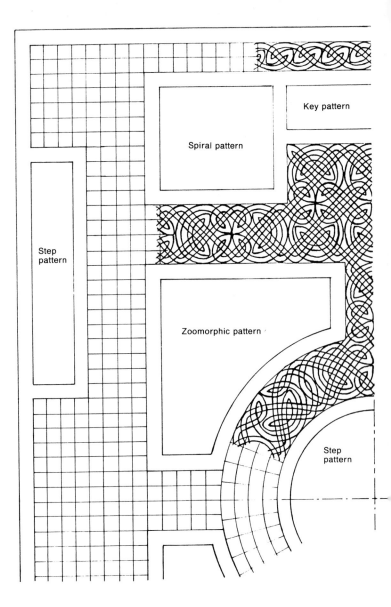

Key pattern

Spiral pattern

Step
pattern

Zoomorphic pattern

Step
pattern

This is the layout for a quarter of the full-page design in the *Lindisfarne Gospels*, folio 94b (Plate 1), showing the grid for the knotwork, with some of the pattern sketched in. The layout was chosen to suit a square grid, and it could have been decided before choosing the particular knotwork patterns because the grid divides into a whole number of grid-units, and will accommodate a variety of knotwork patterns.

Plate 1. Folio 94b from the *Lindisfarne Gospels*

Plate 2. Folio 95 from the *Lindisfarne Gospels*

The grid does not contribute to the final lines of the pattern. However, in addition to subdividing the pattern space correcly it provides good guidelines for the remaining setting-out of the pattern, including the diagonals which do contribute to the final lines.

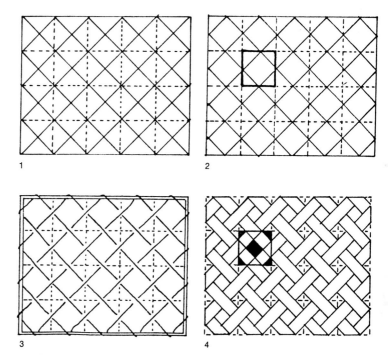

1 The obvious way to impose diagonals on an enclosed grid is to draw them through the grid crossing-points. But trace their paths (in this case two) crossing one another and bouncing off the sides, and you will find that they always come to an end in a corner. Note also that the diagonals divide every square grid-unit into four triangles.

2 If, however, the diagonals are drawn through the mid-points of the lines making each grid-unit, their path (in this case only one) is not trapped in the corners and now becomes endless. Note also that the diagonals divide every grid-unit into one lozenge and four triangles, as outlined in figure 2. This is the *Centre-line Cell*.

3 The figure can be redrawn to represent a continuous cord stretched over a frame and interwoven at the crossings; a kind of angular plait.

4 Or it can be re-drawn to represent a strip of paper, folded and interwoven so that the width of paper is the same as the distance between the strips. The basic unit, repeated in every grid-unit, is picked out in figure 4 with a dark background. It is the basic construction unit for most Celtic knotwork patterns. I call it the *Grid Cell*.

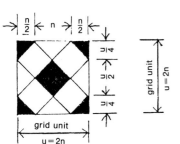

The Grid Cell

The background is dark.

u is the grid-unit measurement.

n is the diagonal spacing, measured horizontally or vertically.

The diagonal lines meet the grid lines at the quarter-points, and n equals $\frac{u}{2}$. The centre must be empty.

Note that in these methods the term 'Grid Cell' means the quarter-point cell, in which the cord thickness is equal to the space between cords. The Centre-line Cell, and the Wide-cord Cell in Chapter 9, are described thus.

Angular plaits can be constructed wholly from the Grid Cell:

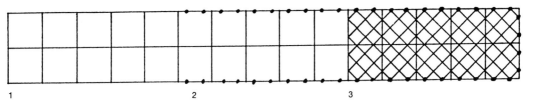

1 Draw the grid.
2 Mark the quarter-points.
3 Draw the diagonals.

4 In each grid-unit darken the △s in the corners and the ◇ in the middle.
5 Erase all lines within the strips.
6 Redraw strip edges to form the interlacing. The order reverses from axis to axis.

Angular knotwork can be formed with very little adjustment.

For *Lindisfarne* folio 12, seen in Chapter 1, break and rejoin vertically at points X (or alternately on axes 1 and 3 every third crossing).

The rendering at the top of page 27 shows the likeness to a folded and interwoven strip of paper. If you trace its path you will find there is only one strip.

Note that the pattern is achieved merely by erasing some of the Stage 4 setting-out lines.

axis 1

axis 2

axis 3

For *Lindisfarne* folio 94b, seen in Chapter 1, break and rejoin the basic plait vertically at points Y (on axis 2 at crossings 1, 3, 5, etc.) and horizontally at points Z (alternately on axes 3 and 1 at every crossing).

With some extra folding, the paper-strip analogy still applies. Again there is only one strip.

The setting-out diagrams in this angular form begin to resemble Celtic patterns merely by the substitution of curves for angled bends in the final rendering, as illustrated below:

But if curves are to be drawn there is no point in providing diagonal setting-out lines where these most often occur, which in Celtic patterns is in the margins. Hence the setting-out methods which are outlined in Chapter 1 and continued in Chapter 3.

The geometry of the Grid Cell

The fact that grid-units are not necessarily square does not affect the setting-out of the Grid Cells. The diagonals still meet the grid sides at the quarter-points. The final lines in a Celtic knotwork design do not necessarily coincide with the setting-out lines, because the pattern produced by the setting-out lines need do no more than provide guidelines for the free expression of the final design. Furthermore, the setting-out lines themselves are not dependent on exact geometry. It is because it provides guidelines only that the square Grid Cell is so valuable, and proves a rapid vehicle for the production of a vast range of Celtic knotwork patterns.

The selection of patterns to fit into chosen spaces and their transfer to these is easily achieved because of the variability of the Grid Cell.

Conversely it is because Celtic patterns are not slaves to the square or the rectangle that they can be independent of geometry. Using a square grid, Celtic patterns could, with tedium, be drawn geometrically and accurately with circular curves, and indeed this might be justifiable for large-scale guidelines on stone, but the likelihood is that truly geometric patterns would be as boring to look at as to execute. The same would apply in the case of a rectangular grid, which would be even more tedious to draw geometrically. However, by adopting the approximate geometry of the Celts to draw the curves, grid-units can be distorted at will and yet still provide suitable guidelines for the final execution of a satisfying design.

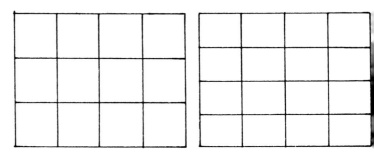

The square is the *optimum* shape of grid-unit. Though the panels above are the same size, the one on the left has fewer grid-units because these are square. Rectangular grid-units are usually as seen above, with horizontal (h) exceeding vertical (v) in length. This means that sometimes a pattern may appear sideways or even upside-down, for example if used to border a page.

The cells within a square grid

Consider the simplest versions of figures 3 and 4 on page 25.

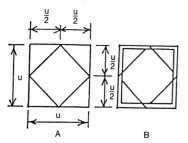

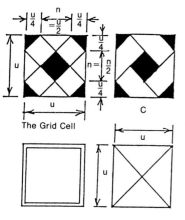

The Grid Cell

Figure A is a diagrammatic version of figure B, which represents a continuous thin string stretched round a square frame.

The Grid Cell is the diagrammatic version of figure C which represents a continuous strip of paper folded within a square. The width of the strip is such that all the diagonals meet the grid sides at the quarter-points. The centre must be empty.

But figures B and C represent only two specific widths of material. Make the string thinner until its thickness is zero, and the frame will be empty. At the other end of the scale, widen the strip of paper and eventually it will fill the whole square.

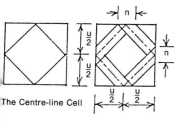

The Centre-line Cell

In the Centre-line Cell the diagonals in figure A are taken to represent the centre-lines of cords of any width n between zero and u. I can find little evidence of the use of the Centre-line Cell in construction, apart from examples on pages 99 and 100, using a 3:4 grid. Some notes on the Centre-line Cell also appear on page 100.

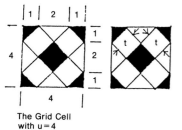

The Grid Cell
with u = 4

The Grid Cell within a square grid is unique: the horizontal and vertical values of u and n are the same; the diagonals slope at an angle of 45 degrees, and all are equally spaced. In the 4 × 4 grid n equals 2 and t (the actual thickness of the cords) equals 0.707n, or 1.414.

During the preparation of this book the advantages of using a Wide-cord Cell to set out wide-cord and *Lindisfarne* double-interlaced finishing treatments became apparent. Construction-methods using this Wide-cord Cell appear in Chapter 9.

Cells within a grid which is not square

The Grid Cell diagonals still meet the quarter-points of the grid sides, and the Centre-line Cell diagonals still meet the mid-points of the grid sides. The Grid Cells control the drawing of the curves, but if the geometry of the curves is approximate, there seems no reason why the grid sides should not vary in size, or even be curved instead of straight.

Below is a selection of quadrilateral grid-units.

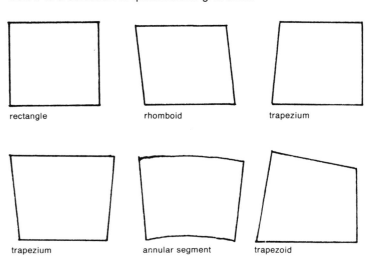

rectangle   rhomboid   trapezium

trapezium   annular segment   trapezoid

All quadrilateral shapes other than the square and rectangle have one or more sides which are neither horizontal nor vertical, but these are of no consequence in the design stage of construction, which uses the square grid, or occasionally the 3 × 4 rectangle. Distortion occurs only when adapting a chosen design to a chosen space which will not divide into square or rectangular grid-units. As will be shown later, this adaptation is not difficult.

The 3 × 4 grid:

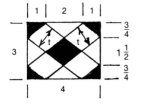

The Grid Cell

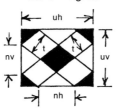

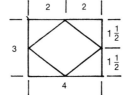

The Centre-line Cell

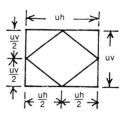

The vertical (v) values of u and n are now different from their horizontal (h) values. The actual thickness of the cords (t) and the spaces between, which in the 4 × 4 square grid cell is 1.414, becomes 1.2 ($1\frac{1}{5}$). This is derived from the 3:4:5 triangle, being $\frac{3}{5}$ of 2(nh) or $\frac{4}{5}$ of $\frac{3}{2}$(nv).

Thus as the slope angle in the Grid Cell flattens, the cord becomes thinner, but at the same time it thickens in relation to the vertical grid spacing.

If the grid-unit is neither square nor rectangular, the cord thickness will vary.

The rhomboid, or parallelogram, contains diagonal cords of different thickness. In a trapezium, the cords are tapered and continue to be so as grid-units reduce in size in a tapered panel. In the annular unit the cords are curved as well as tapered.

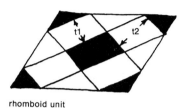

rhomboid unit

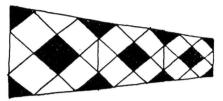

trapezoid units

annular unit

The effect of such variations in a setting-out diagram can be adjusted when carrying out the finishing treatment, or accepted without adjustment if desired.

Examples of irregular panels appear in Chapters 8, 9 and 10, and a good example using the rhombus is on the *Book of Kells* folio 290V (Plate 8), which is reconstructed on page 81.

Chapter 3

The Curves

As stated in Chapter 2, dispense with diagonal setting-out lines in margins of the pattern where curves are expected to appear. Proceed, therefore, as in Chapter 1, but for a change use a grid 3u wide and 4u long. At this stage ignore the geometry of the curves.

The construction stages are repeated to stress them:

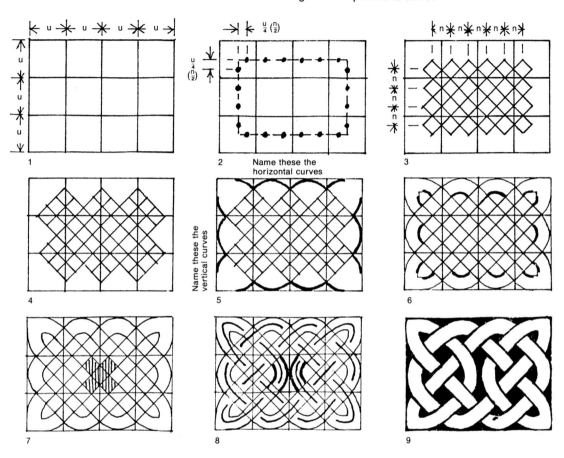

1 Draw the grid.
2 Draw the margin and mark the quarter points.
3 Draw the diagonals.
4 Extend those diagonals which meet at the grid lines (at the quarter points).
5 Draw the outer curves.
6 Draw the inner curves, and the short straight lines in the corners. Maintain constant cord thickness.

That completes the basic plait. Continue with the knotwork.

7 Make one break in the middle
8 Re-join vertically. Roughly mark the overs and unders.
9 Apply the final treatment freehand, adjusting the curves as may be desired.

All linework to stage 8 is setting-out. The only erasure necessary is for the break in stage 7. It is helpful to impress the diagonal and grid lines in stage 3 with a stylus (or knitting needle). Different breaks can then be tried.

The previous figure uses only the short curve described in Chapter 1.
The long curve in Chapter 1 evolves from the short curve thus:

Name these the
horizontal curves.

Name these the vertical curves.

1 Erase the hatched area.
2 Rejoin with a straight length of cord. The spots indicate the ends of the 45° short curves.
3 Change the springing points and sweep the long curves through 90°.
  Use in the 3u by 4u grid:
4 Draw the grid and diagonals (stage 3 on page 32).
5 Draw 90° long curves top and bottom, and 45° long curves on the sides as shown.
6 Link up with short curves in the corners.
7 Link up the inner cords on each side with short curves.
8 Link up the inner cords top and bottom with curves sprung from the same diagonals as the long curves. Roughly mark the overs and unders to complete the setting-out diagram.
9 The setting-out lines themselves flow sweetly. Here the cords have been slightly thickened in the final treatment.

The above pattern introduces the occasionally used 'middle' curve. It sometimes replaces the short curve, as here, where it is used concentrically with the long curve.

These two examples are typical of the vast range of patterns which evolve from the grid and the plait. To reconstruct existing patterns, long curves can be drawn directly, as shown above. To create patterns it is simpler to draw the whole plait (figure 6 on page 32) and substitute long curves by trial. This is when stylus-impressed grid and diagonal lines are helpful.

The approximate geometry of the curves

An important feature of this method of construction is that aid in the drawing of curved cords is provided for each of eight arcs of a circle. Unless the grid is square, i.e. unless the slope of the diagonals is 45°, half the arcs will cover more, and the other half less, than one-eighth of a circle. But in practice this is of no significance, so that in all cases each arc can be regarded as nominally covering one-eighth of a circle. Indeed, when curves continue beyond one-eighth of a circle, it is helpful to regard them as being subdivided into one-eighth of a circle arcs.

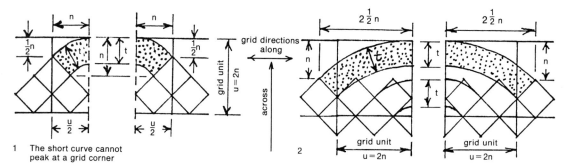

1   The short curve cannot peak at a grid corner

2

Note: Within a square grid only, t (the cord thickness) equals 0.7n.

1   The short curve moves 1n along and $\frac{1}{2}$n across.

2   The long curve moves $2\frac{1}{2}$n along and 1n across. It is shown with the short curve below as often drawn.

The same rules apply even when the grid is not square. They apply wherever the curves appear in the pattern, not just in the margins, and the curves may be turned sideways or upside-down. The only exception is the cord thickness, see page 30 and opposite.

Always remember that it is the outer lines of the curves which are defined. The inner lines are drawn by maintaining a constant cord thickness, t, which for one-eighth circle control can be taken as $\frac{3}{4}$n. This can be expressed as the $t = \frac{3}{4}$n rule.

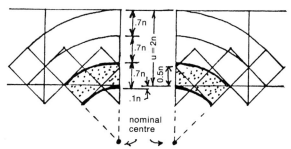

The middle curve, sometimes drawn below the long curve.

The middle curve follows the same sweep as the long curve. If drawn with compasses, it would use the same centre.

Within a square grid, and only then, 3t is 3 × 0.7n or 2.1n. The 0.7n cord straddles the 0.5n grid points as shown above, thus providing one-eighth circle control for the middle curve.

In Celtic knotwork the slope angle is seldom less than 37° which is that of the 3:4:5 triangle. Therefore in a rectangular grid the constant cord thickness ranges between 0.7n (square grid) and 0.8nv or 0.6nh (3:4 grid). But the $t = \frac{3}{4}n$ rule does not fully apply when the grid is not square, as is shown below:

Square Grid Cell   3:4 Grid Cell

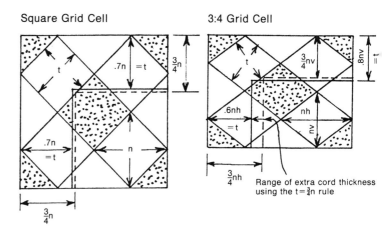

Range of extra cord thickness using the $t = \frac{3}{4}n$ rule

In finishing all three examples of this simple pattern the curves have been rounded off.

Square grid

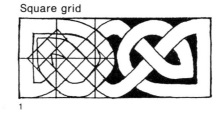

1

3:4 grid   3:4 grid

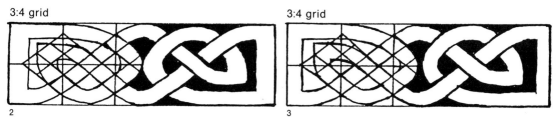

2   3

1 No thickness adjustment required.
2 Unadjusted. Cords thicker at horizontal control points. The shapes in figure 2 are not displeasing.
3 Constant cord thickness adjustment.

At the scale of the Grid Cells the thicker vertical component of the cords is significant, but not so at the scale of the patterns. It is convenient to use the $\frac{3}{4}n$ rule for all grid shapes, particularly the irregular ones which are judged by eye alone (see Chapter 8).
The choice of adjustment is always available at the finishing stage.
The middle curve (not shown) moves downwards gridwise as it flattens, but following the long curve helps to locate it.

So far the only guidance on the shape of curves has been to subdivide them into one-eighth of a circle arcs, and to avoid kinks or reverse curves. Doing this should produce curves which are tangential to the grid and diagonal lines. A tangent meets a circle at one point only, and at that point the angle between the radius of the circle and the tangent is 90°.

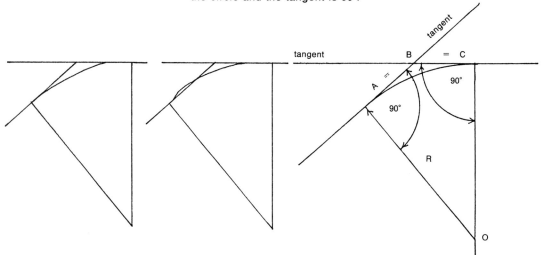

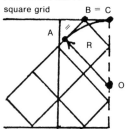

The short curve

square grid

If you have been testing the constructions in Chapter 1 and at the start of this chapter, and have found that whereas the long curve flowed easily the short curve did not, this is because the short curve seems to peak more than a circular curve would do between the same two points. The reason is that tangent point A is away from the diagonal junction as illustrated alongside. With practice this is easily corrected by extending the diagonal slightly before sweeping the curve round to join the grid line. Within a square grid the long curve is very nearly correct without adjustment.

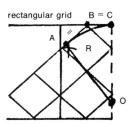

rectangular grid

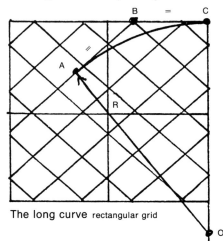

The long curve rectangular grid

If any time you want to find the true centres of the curves, it can be done graphically, as shown above, because B is always on a grid quarter point, AB = BC, and angles BAO and BCO always = 90°.

But beware when the grid is not square. Note what happens to the short and long curve centres with a rectangular grid (B) on page 37. Introducing different diagonals to set out the curves with compasses merely invites confusion.

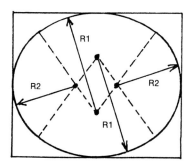

Furthermore the previous diagrams show only horizontal curves (curves on a horizontal base), but as illustrated left the horizontal and vertical curves within a rectangle have different radii.

Romilly Allen said that the Celtic designer never used more geometry than he could possibly help. Yet any attempt to explain the geometric derivation of these construction-methods immediately breaks that rule, and makes complications out of simplicity. For this reason the geometric construction of the curves is set out below without comment, except to repeat that all work to this stage is setting-out only. Dotted lines show how the long outer curve could be sweetened in the final treatment.

A Square grid

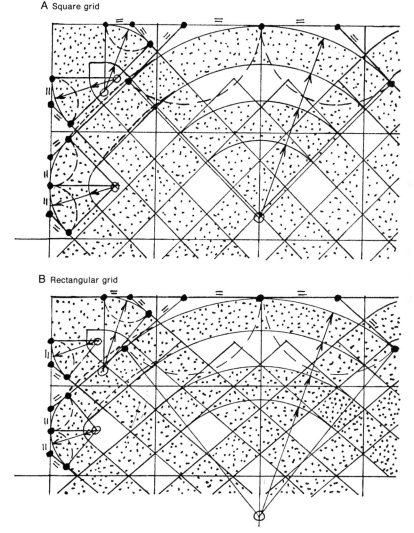

B Rectangular grid

Note how the middle curve moves down gridwise.
We can now resume the approximate geometry.

Chapter 4
The Plait and the Interlacing

The Plait

A plait, the basis of virtually all Celtic knotwork, can be described as a cut-out from an overall spread of grid cells, the cut cords being rejoined with short curves.

1 A 3u wide by 4u long cut-out.
2 The same with the cords rejoined top and bottom. A six-cord plait is thus formed, whichever cross section is chosen for the count.
3 The same but with the cords rejoined at the sides, thus forming an eight-cord plait.

Rejoin the cords all round, and a closed plait is formed. It can be expressed as either a six-cord horizontal plait or an eight-cord vertical plait. In either aspect the number of cords is twice the number of grid-units. Thus the 3u × 4u figure is a 6 × 8 cord plait, but unless the length is significant it is usually sufficient to name it by width alone.

Strangely in this 6-cord plait all the cords join together to form one path. Not all such figures have only one path: figures with the same number of cords in each direction have half of that number of paths, counting half a path in the answer as a whole. For example:

a 4 × 4 plait has 2 paths

a 5 × 5 plait has 3 paths

a 6 × 6 plait has 3 paths

(But note that the arithmetic is correct if a path which does not return to its origin is regarded as half a path.)

Plaited figures have only one path unless the number of cords in each direction has a common divisor greater than two. Thus:

A 3 × 6 plait has 2 paths (divisor 3)

A 4 × 6 plait has 1 path (divisor 2)

A 4 × 8 plait has 2 paths (divisor 4)

It would be inconceivable for anyone devising knotwork patterns not to attach symbolic significance to the single endless path, although in Celtic art such continuity was not always insisted upon. This may have been because preference was sometimes given to design detail when the choice was between this and continuity of path.

These simple rules of continuity of path do not apply, however, when the cords in a basic plait are broken and rejoined to form knotwork, as illustrated below:

In the 3 × 6 plait, 1 break makes 1 path.

In the 4 × 6 plait, 1 break makes 2 paths.

In the 4 × 8 plait, 1 break makes 1 path.

More consideration of the intriguing subject of continuity of path appears on page 55, but some reference should be made here to those plaits with an odd number of cords, like the 3- and 5-cord plaits introduced in this chapter. Knotwork patterns evolved from these rarely occur in Celtic art because the ends cannot be fully closed, but there is no reason why they should not be used where continuity can be provided, as in borders which form a complete surround, or in any other situation where the loose ends can be accommodated. The simplest example is the Stafford knot shown below:

Note that if plaits with an odd number of cords have the loose cords joined together they become even numbered.

3-cord plait.

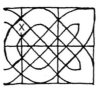

The loose ends joined.

X axis

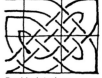

4-cord plait.

Figure 2 is derived from figure 3 by making horizontal breaks on the X–X axis.

An interesting use of the loose ends of a 5-cord plait appears in the *Lindisfarne Gospels*, folio 138b:

In a 4 × 5 plait, make a horizontal break at x

Double interlace

The whole forms a bird's tail feathers

Strictly speaking a closed plait is not a plait, because pairing the cords reduces their number, and shortening or thickening the cords forms a knot or a knot-like figure. It is, however, convenient to think of the closed plait as representing on one drawing each of the two plaits which could be formed from a cut-out, as shown on page 38.

The unclosed version of the 3 × 8 cord plait.

The unclosed version of the 4 × 8 plait.

The closed version has one cord which can be pulled tight. (Odd-numbered plaits may be regarded as closed if only the odd cords are loose.)

The knot-like closed version has two cords.

Confusion regarding the number of cords can be avoided by referring to the number of paths they trace.

Plate 3. Folio 291V from the *Book of Kells*

Plate 4. Folio 21V from the *Book of Durrow*

The Interlacing

In single-interlacing, the overs and unders are the same on each axis, horizontal and vertical, and they reverse from axis to axis. In double-interlacing the overs and unders are the same on each mini-axis, and they reverse from mini-axis to mini-axis. They are, however, the same at every double crossing.

Single

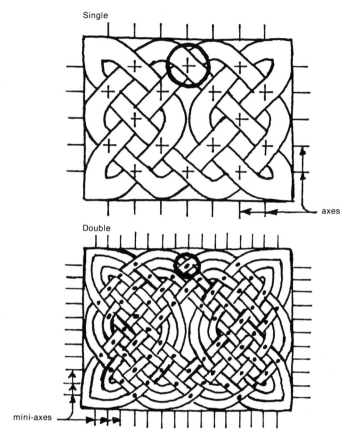

axes

Double

mini-axes

Some distinction is needed between the over and under cords, and the following annotation is used here, referring to the uppermost marginal crossings (ringed on the diagrams above).

right-handed

left-handed

The single-interlaced pattern is therefore right-handed and the double-interlaced pattern is left-handed. Rotating the pattern sideways or upside-down makes no difference, since each viewing aspect provides the same answer.

Most *Lindisfarne* interlacing, single or double, is left-handed, but other sources, including *Kells* and *Durrow* and the stone carvings, use both orders – both sometimes appearing in different panels on the same page or carving. The choice, therefore, is purely personal.

'Knotwork' is the term used to describe the appearance of loose knots caused by breaking and re-pairing some of the cords in a plait. The phrase 'appearance of loose knots' is used because the figures thus formed are not necessarily capable of being tied.

We have seen in Chapter 4 that a closed plait is itself a knot, which can be simple or complex, as seen in the cross.

The cords need not form one path, as they do here. But each figure is unbroken, in the knotwork sense, until breaks, (henceforth assumed to include re-pairings) are introduced to the plain interlacing.

A knotwork version of the 3 × 8 cord plait.

This rendering of the cross appears double-interlaced on *Kells* folio 29IV (Plate 3), see page 85.

Note another two crosses formed by the background where the pointed spades meet.

Discounting a few examples of random breaks on some interlaced monumental carvings, knotwork breaks were arranged to create recognizable patterns.

They were sometimes used sparingly, as below:

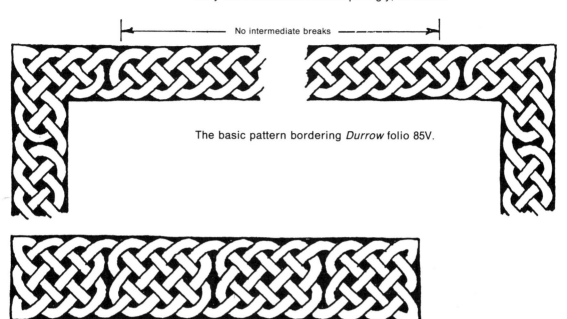

The basic pattern bordering *Durrow* folio 85V.

The basic pattern in the capital T on *Kells* folio 124R.

Sometimes they were used lavishly in repetition.

This basic pattern, popular in *Lindisfarne*, including folio 27, also illustrates the illusory nature of Celtic knotwork. It has three different 'looks' depending on whether the eye rests on A, B or the background crosses as at C.

The pattern can evolve from the 3 × 5 cord plait:

1 Mirror vertically.
2 Re-plait the cords where spotted.
3 Mirror horizontally.

This can also make an overall pattern, as shown on page 59.

Romilly Allen isolated the following eight knots which are reconstructed here as setting-out exercises. There is no need to memorize their numbers, which are not Romilly Allen's.

The grid markings around the edges are for emphasis.

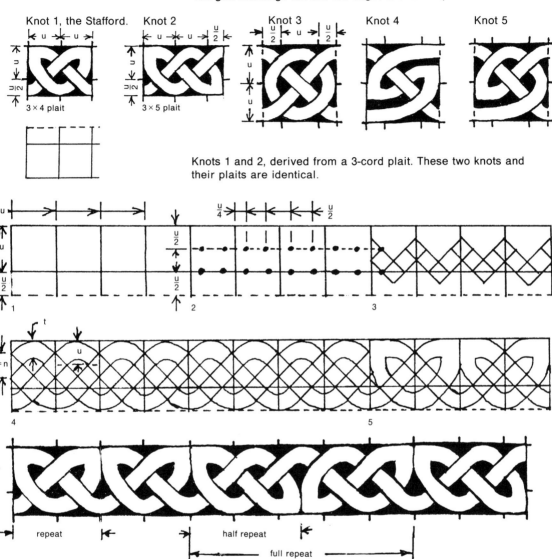

Knot 1, the Stafford.   Knot 2   Knot 3   Knot 4   Knot 5

3 × 4 plait   3 × 5 plait

Knots 1 and 2, derived from a 3-cord plait. These two knots and their plaits are identical.

repeat   half repeat   full repeat

1 Draw the 1.5u grid. The grid may be either way up.
2 Mark the margin and spot the quarter-points.
3 Because a plait has only short curves, the diagonals may be extended into the margin. They meet at the side of full grid-units and within half grid-units.
4 Draw the short curves to complete the plait. To maintain cord thickness, guess t by eye as $\frac{3}{4}$n.
5 Form vertical breaks in one margin at every other crossing for the Stafford knot. Mark the interlacing.

Knot 1 repeats every two grid-units.

For Knot 2, alternate the vertical breaks from one margin to the other. Knot 2 repeats fully every five grid-units.

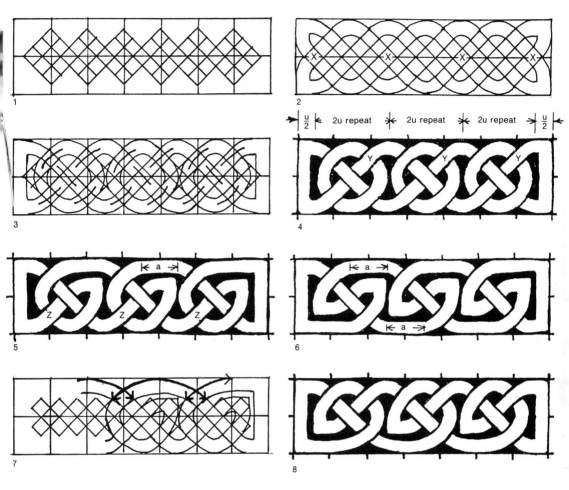

1 Draw a 2u grid which is an odd number of units long, and fill in the diagonals. These may be continued into the margin.
2 Draw the short curves all around to form the plait. Ignore the interlacing.
3 Make vertical breaks at X in Figure 2. Mark the interlacing.
4 The completed repeating Knot 3. Breaks do not disturb the interlacing.
5 Horizontal breaks at Y in Figure 4 produce a version of repeating Knot 4. 'a' is straight.
6 Horizontal breaks at Z in Figure 5 produce a version of repeating Knot 5. 'a' is straight.
 These versions are acceptable, but introducing the long curve to the spiral gives a smoother flow, as shown below:
7 The extension of the diagonals into the margin is unnecessary if long curves are anticipated in the pattern. Note how the inner lines of the cord-returns meet at a diagonal.
8 Knot 4 with long curves outside the short curves. You may have realized that the long-curved version of Knot 5 appears in the outline in Chapter 1.

Knot 6

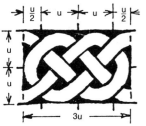

Knot 7

Knot 8

Knot 6 repeated. As for Knot 3, break the 2u plait vertically on the middle axis, but at every third intersection.

Knot 7 repeated. Knot 7 is obtained by breaking Knot 6 vertically at X.

Knot 8 repeated. Knot 8 is obtained by breaking Knot 6 horizontally at Y, and substituting long for short curves in the margin.

This repeating Knot 8 was less favoured by the Celts than the extended version shown below, with the breaks recurring every fourth intersection. The likely reason is that, unlike the upper version, the lower version has a continuous path. These knots in fact contain clues to the rules governing continuity of path, which appear on page 55.

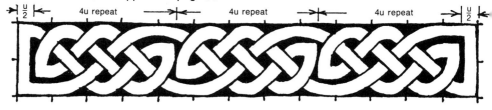

Some of these knots can be drawn with different aspects, the most versatile being Knot 4 which can be mirrored both vertically and horizontally.

Other knots can be extended like Knot 8 to give patterns with more than the minimum repeat. Knot 8 is in fact an extended Knot 5, and Knot 6 is an extended Knot 3. Extension is achieved by introducing additional short curve (plait) units, either at full- or mid-grid positions. Extensions to Knots 1 to 7 are illustrated below:

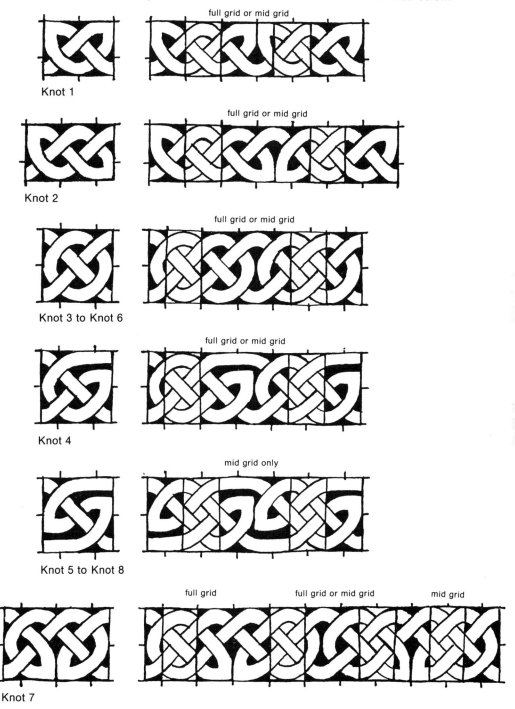

Knot 1

Knot 2

Knot 3 to Knot 6

Knot 4

Knot 5 to Knot 8

Knot 7

Short curves and straights are used instead of long curves in theory, but not necessarily in practice.

There may be other knots which could be added to Romilly Allen's eight. Two certainly are worth mentioning: number these 9 and 10.

Knot 9

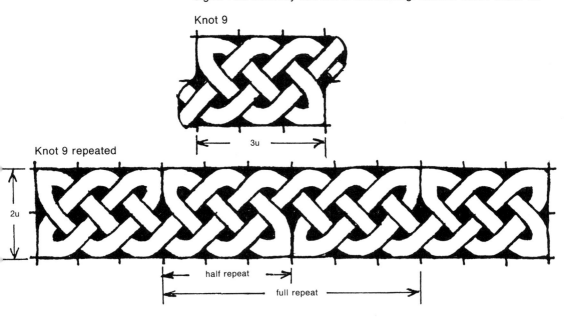

Knot 9 repeated

2u

3u

half repeat

full repeat

This is the 2u version of Knot 2 which appears in the *Lindisfarne Gospels*, folio 12, and is described in the outline in Chapter 1.

The other is the long curve version of the ring Knot 3.

Knot 10

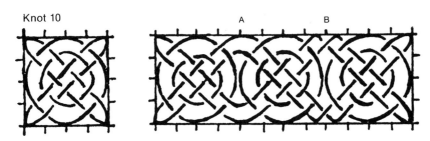

A   B

Knot 10 resembles a double-interlaced version of Knot 3. The knot can be repeated by connecting as at either A or B.

Doubling the cords has the effect of doubling the grid-units, so that there are no half units at the ends. These can therefore be closed by joining the loose cords.

The detailed construction of Knot 10 using long and middle curves is given opposite.

The construction of Knot 10 introduces the full-circle long curve which is the basis of circular knotwork like the pattern on *Lindisfarne* folio 94b (Plate 1).

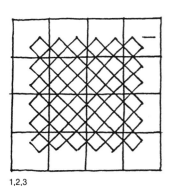

1,2,3

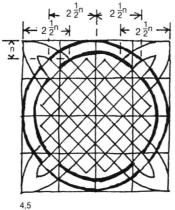

4,5

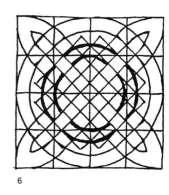

6

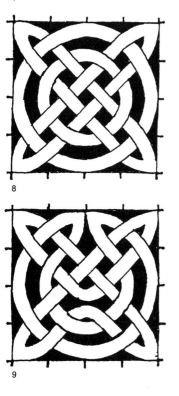

7

8

9

1 Draw a 4u by 4u grid.
2 Mark the $\frac{1}{4}$ points around the margin.
3 Draw the diagonals.
4 Draw the outer lines of the long curves.
5 Follow with their inner lines. Note: the corner curves may be either short or long.
6 Draw the concentric middle curve. Note how the lines straddle grid and diagonal crossings.
7 Mark the overs and unders.
8 Knot 10.
9 See how two breaks make a 'horseshoe' pattern.

The eccentric short curve
Of Knots 1 to 10, all but 9 and 10 have half grid-units in their construction, and joining these causes pattern repeats at mid-grid positions. This is due to the eccentric short curve, and is illustrated by this overall ring pattern which requires half grid closures on two sides.

See also pages 55 and 56.

Any pattern classification would be complicated by the mid-grid
repeats and the different pattern 'looks'. This is illustrated by Knot 7:

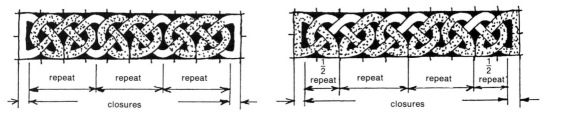

The inventive *Book of Durrow* has on folio 124V (Plate 5) what can
only be described as a stepped repeat:

End closures have been added to this standard rendering.

The Celts were not always consistent in their use of knotwork.
There are examples of adjustments made to avoid running out of
space, changes of pattern for no apparent reason, and the apparent
disregard of otherwise consistently kept customs. More knowledge
of the subject might reveal good reasons for these seeming
anomalies. Some may be explained as being adjustment to correct
cumulative errors occurring during the final application of pigments,
but I find it difficult to subscribe to the theory of delegation of work
to inferior scribes or artists. A more likely answer would be a
humble reluctance to presume to perfection in work executed for
the eyes of God.

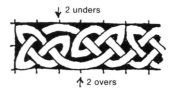

Surely the scribe Eadfrith's interlacing mistakes were deliberate on
Lindisfarne folio 11b?

Here is one pattern inconsistency, however, for which there is a
valid reason – a pattern on *Lindisfarne* folio 95 (Plate 2).
This standard rendering looks wrong with the break shown spotted,
but it has only one path. Re-form the plait to balance the pattern
and it would have two paths.

Romilly Allen classified hundreds of these knots or knot-like patterns, but no attempt is made to do so here. We have already seen how the eye can be drawn to different aspects of the same knot and how there can be knots within knots.

Examples of how knots can be mixed, multiplied, rotated, mirrored, and otherwise varied appear elsewhere in this book, and although these and many many more could be created and stored (this even by computer, using polar co-ordinates), it could be argued that this is neither necessary nor desirable.

The reader will find that by practising the reconstruction of existing patterns, familiarity with the knotwork language will quickly increase, until creation will become doodling within subconsciously controlled parameters. But do not be surprised if, like the author, at some later date you find that your 'creations' were already in existence over a thousand years ago.

Side of cross-shaft, No 4,
Monifieth, Tayside

Cross-shaft at Kirk of Norham, Northumberland

Chapter 6
Knotwork characteristics

A striking feature of Celtic knotwork is the similarity of form and proportions, all peculiar to the art, and all evolved from the plait, which underlie the different finishing treatments favoured in the Celtic world. In the case of the stone carvings and the *Lindisfarne Gospels* and the *Book of Kells* the similarities are quite apparent, but not so in the *Book of Durrow*, in which the knotwork has its own particular finishing treatment, and also seems to be a baffling mixture of the simple and complex. The fact that these complex patterns also evolve from plaits, and very simple ones at that, seems to confirm the existence of a common cultural bond throughout the Celtic world.

The following examples illustrate these similarities and differences.

This is drawn 3:4. The original is slightly flatter. This combines Knots 4 and 5.

From *Kells* folio 3R:

In double-interlacing the edge lines into cords, they have been kept as thin lines. These are yellow on a dark background.

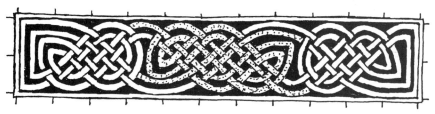

The grid is square. The knots are extended versions of Knots 4 and 8.

From *Lindisfarne* folio 95 (Plate 2):

The double-interlaced cords are thicker, much the same as the spaces between. The cords are yellow and red on a black background. The spots indicate the red area.

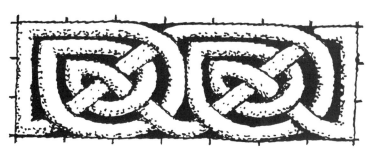

The 3u grid is 3:4. The single-interlacing has a spiral look. The standard pattern is on page 108.

A pattern on a Scottish stone from Monifieth, Tayside (page 52).

From *Durrow* folio 125V (Plate 6):

This repeating knot, here shown with simple end treatment, is part of a rectangular border design. The areas shown dotted are in bright colours, the tight loops in green and the outer cords in alternating red and yellow. Although at first glance the knot looks similar to the red knot from *Lindisfarne* folio 95, it is quite different. A reconstruction appears on pages 82 and 83.

Yet the underlying form and proportions of *Durrow* patterns are consistent with those in other manuscripts and stone carvings, under the following headings:

1 The strong diagonals.
2 The pointed spade look.
3 The consistency of the interlacing.
4 The pattern repeats.
5 The significance of, but not insistence upon, continuity of path.
6 The spiral look.
7 The eccentric short curve.

1 *The strong diagonals*
This characteristic is not confined to the knotwork form of Celtic art. It is dominant also in the key and zoomorphic forms, and in many of the step patterns.

2 *The pointed spade look*
Seen on all four previous examples, this is caused by the strong diagonals and the pointed cord returns.

3 *The consistency of the interlacing*
In all four examples, each 'over' is followed by an 'under'. This is so consistent in Celtic art that rare exceptions must be regarded as errors, albeit perhaps deliberate ones (see pages 50 and 108).

4 *The pattern repeat*
All four examples have knots which are or could be repeated to extend the pattern.

5 *Continuity of path*
This is also seen in all four examples. The very concept of knotwork suggests continuity: clearly this was sought, and it characterizes even intricate patterns; but it was not insisted upon. At the other extreme, rings, or linked cord-returns, whether these cross one or more interlacing cords, should be avoided unless they form an integral part of the pattern order (see Knot 10 and the overall pattern on page 49).

The following rendering of Romilly Allen's Knot 4 shows an unacceptable ring:

1 An unacceptable ring

2 An acceptable solution

3 An acceptable use of Romilly Allen's Knot 3

A partial rule for continuity of path
Two-cord links between knots: to check if the cords form a single path, divide a pattern into knots between vertical breaks. If no cords are confined within the knots at either closed end, and if in each intermediate knot each cord enters at one side and leaves at the other, the pattern will have only one path.

Four-cord links between knots: applying the same rule, the pattern may have one *or* two paths. If there are two paths it is only necessary to break and rejoin the cords where these paths cross. This can be done once at any suitable crossing, or by terminating one end of the pattern at a place where the two paths cross. Both methods are illustrated below, using the continuous version of the *Lindisfarne* folio 95 pattern shown on page 50.

The break at X was the scribe's method. Terminating the pattern Y is an alternative method.

This rule is perhaps helpful for spotting breaks in continuity.

6 *The spiral look*
This comes from the pointed spade unwinding, as is evidenced by Knot 4 in the rendering shown above, Nos 1 and 2. It appears in all examples except the *Lindisfarne* one.

7 *The eccentric short curve* (see also page 49)
This is seen in all four examples. The short-curve ring, Knot 3, occupies the same area as 4 grid-units, but has to straddle 6 grid-units, i.e. 2u × 3u. This is necessary to keep the diagonals clear of the grid centres and corners (see overleaf).

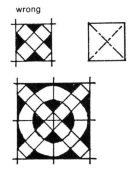
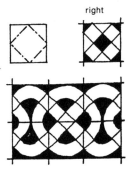

| The cords cover the Grid Cell centres and corners. (The cord centre-line diagonals meet the grid in the corners.) | The Grid Cell centres and corners are empty. (The cord centre-line diagonals meet the grid sides at the mid-points.) |

Also, the short-curve ring is too small to be broken and rejoined within itself.

The long curve, however, completes a ring, Knot 10, within a 4u by 4u grid. Within this ring the short curve must be eccentric:

| The concentric short-curve ring, wrongly placed in the space adjacent to the middle curve and the diagonal cord-returns. | The eccentric short curve ring, rightly placed in one of its 4 possible positions. The centres of these are spotted. |

Note that in all 4 positions the short curve is symmetrical with the long curve relative to the same horizontal or vertical axis.

Breaking the short-curve circle introduces the eccentric look and livens these patterns in which it is emphasized. It is not as noticeable in the *Durrow* example, which has less background between the cords.

The best illustration is perhaps the repeating Knot 5, which was commonly used by the Celts, and is reprinted here from Chapter 1.

Chapter 7
Standard Knotwork

Standard knotwork is drawn on a square grid using the Grid Cell with single-interlacing. Most Celtic patterns can be expressed in this form. (However, the whole object of this book would be defeated were readers to confine their use of knotwork to the production of standard patterns.) Many patterns gain nothing by departure from the square grid, and with some, notably circular knotwork, only minor adjustments are possible; but often the square grid imposes unnecessary limitations on the final panel shape.

How much better it is to divide a chosen panel shape into a suitable grid and then fill this with a pattern which has first been drawn in standard form to assess its suitability.

The patterns which follow do not necessarily portray either the grid proportions or the finished rendering of any existing patterns which they illustrate, but all of them provide a sound basis for the final production of truly Celtic art or craft works.

The simplest panel shape is one unit wide and contains only the two cord twist. It is normally used with larger panels, as an appendage or a link.

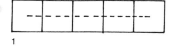
1

1 Draw the grid, say, 5u long. (The 1u panel is all margin.)
2 Spot the quarter-points, including those on the vertical grid lines. Draw the marginal diagonals.
3 Draw the short curved cords. Form a 'spade' at one end. The other end may be left open or closed to a point. Mark the interlacing.
4 Finish off.

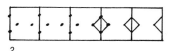
2

3

The twist as a link: a St Andrews, Fife stone carving (page 6).

The twist as an appendage: *Lindisfarne* folio 27.

4

The twist is often used to tail-off patterns within an irregular grid, usually in decorated lettering (see also page 76). The tapered pattern is evolved from rectangular grids:

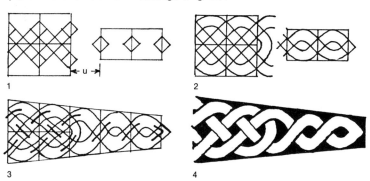

1

2

3

4

1 Draw a 2u and a 1u grid, separated by 1u. Spot the quarter-points and draw the diagonals, extending these to meet the grid lines.
2 Draw the short curves. This completes the standard setting-out.
3 Re-draw figure 2 with non-standard tapered edges. Mark the interlacing.
4 Finish off, adjusting the cord thickness by eye.

The twist and its spade end often appear as part of the pattern in panels wider than one unit:

A corner detail on *Kells* folio 290V (Plate 8).

The pattern on a stone carving at Nevern, Dyfed. The carved cords have their centre-lines incised.

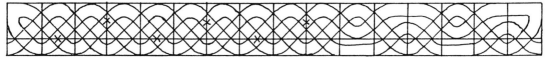

The twist in a 1½u or 3-cord panel.

Draw the 3-cord plait as shown on page 44 with closed ends. Horizontal breaks at X form an interlacing pattern.

The finishing treatment with variations.

Breaks form interesting knotwork:

But loops like these should be avoided.

The loose ends disappear when a complete surround is formed:

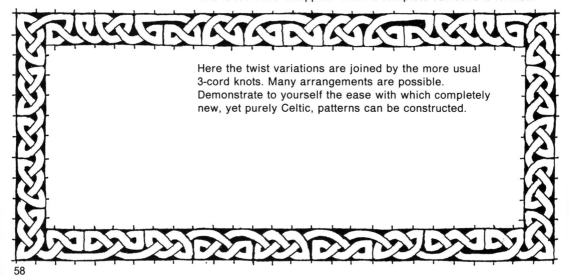

Here the twist variations are joined by the more usual 3-cord knots. Many arrangements are possible. Demonstrate to yourself the ease with which completely new, yet purely Celtic, patterns can be constructed.

Different renderings of the twist in a 2u pattern, formed by breaking the basic plait:

Again there are many arrangements. The split-cord variation below right is on *Durrow* folio 193 r.

Doubling up is an obvious way of widening panels. 1½u patterns can be doubled into 3u panels, 2u into 4u and so on. Some can even be made into overall patterns.

Some 3u arrangements, using Romilly Allen's Knots 1 and 2, with overall versions below:

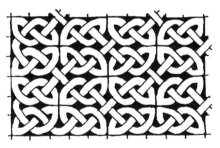

Note on the right that some Stafford knots have had to be broken and re-plaited to provide vertical continuity.

59

Celtic works do not have to be big or complicated. Simple little designs can be equally effective. They can also go astray if the construction stages are taken lightly, as the author knows only too well; and that is one reason for repeating them here:

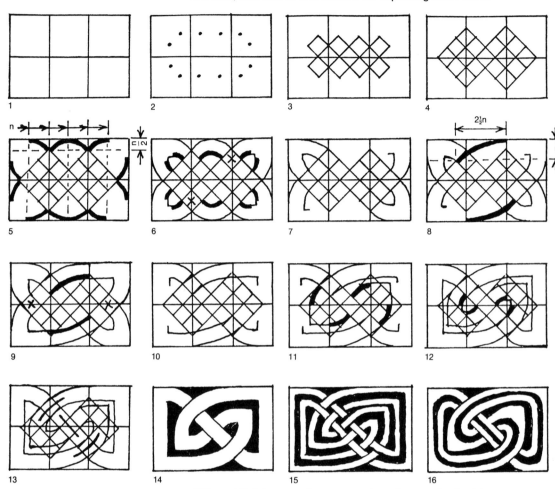

Different finishes can be assessed on the standard grid.

If the grid and diagonals are impressed with a hard pencil or a stylus, the setting-out can be retained while softly drawing and erasing different patterns.

It may encourage the reader to know that the stages repeated above for the drawing of such a small pattern contain virtually all the geometry needed for the largest and most complicated standard pattern. The only exception is the occasionally used middle curve, which poses no problems since it follows the sweep of the long curve (see page 34). More geometry would merely restrict the final panel shape.

A possible final rendering of this single Knot 5.

A great many patterns are possible in panels that are small in terms of grid-units.

Here are several more 2u × 3u patterns:

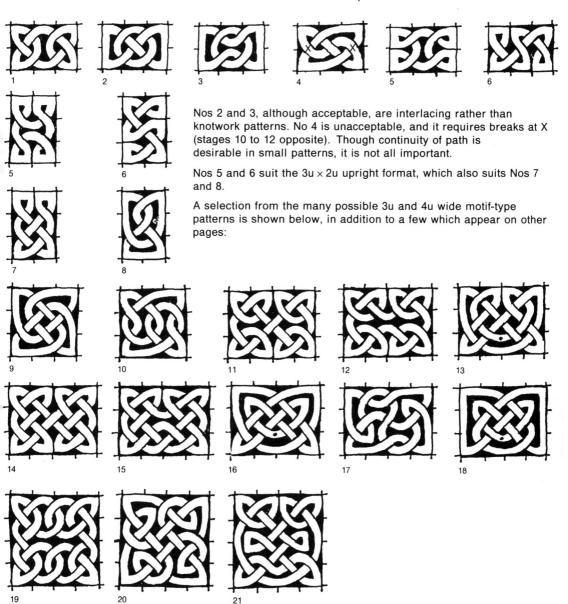

Nos 2 and 3, although acceptable, are interlacing rather than knotwork patterns. No 4 is unacceptable, and it requires breaks at X (stages 10 to 12 opposite). Though continuity of path is desirable in small patterns, it is not all important.

Nos 5 and 6 suit the 3u × 2u upright format, which also suits Nos 7 and 8.

A selection from the many possible 3u and 4u wide motif-type patterns is shown below, in addition to a few which appear on other pages:

A spot indicates that either a short or a middle curve may be used.

See Chapter 12 for standard reconstructions.

The final cords

Which curve?

If the reader, in following these construction-methods, has queried my choice of a short or long curve in various situations, the answer is that very often either can be used.

No choice

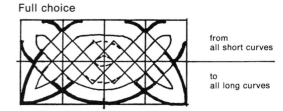

Short curves only.

Full choice

from
all short curves

to
all long curves

Even within the same pattern the choice of curves alone can affect the final appearance:

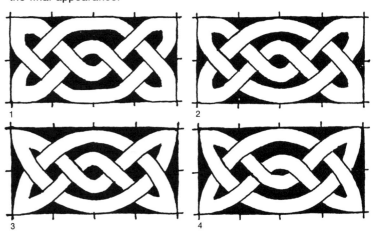

These versions range from the chunky all-short-curve No 1 to the sleek flowing No 4, where the curves on the mid-axis have been flattened almost to middle curves to reduce the short-curve eccentricity. No 2 is the most truly Celtic version, with the long curves on the sides only.

Many patterns get their character from the long curve. They include this 3u *Lindisfarne* pattern and those 4u patterns to which Romilly Allen gave the title 'circular knotwork'.

These appear double-interlaced on *Lindisfarne* folios 95 (Plate 2) and 27 respectively.

The choice of curves often settles itself in the course of sweeping these in during the finishing process. To be sure of achieving a true Celtic 'look', it is helpful to use short curves when in doubt, and to draw the setting-out diagram as accurately as possible. (The final rendering provides plenty of opportunities for inaccuracies to creep in.) Study of the pattern will then suggest adjustments which can be indicated in pencil, or applied directly in the finishing medium.

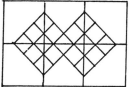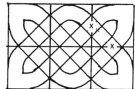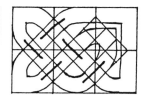

1 A 2u × 3u plait (all short curves), broken at X, finished without adjustment.

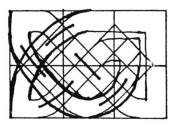

2 The short curves in figure 1 sweetened.

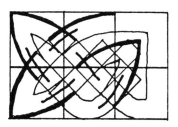

3 The pattern drawn with long curves and no adjustment.

There are other combinations which the reader may try, but the author submits that figure 2 has the Celtic 'look' and is the most satisfying. The same principles apply whatever the grid and panel shapes.

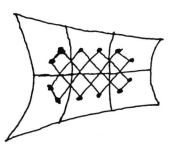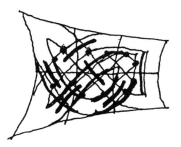

It helps to adjust the cord lines on a draft which has the grid and diagonal lines drawn in ink or hard pencil, or stylus-impressed. Set out the final drawing lightly in soft pencil and adjust with stronger lines. You will find that the interlacing guide marks unravel the bird's nest for the finishing treatment.

Cord line adjustments

In Celtic knotwork the setting-out provides the discipline and the final art-work expresses the freedom. It says much for the pleasing shapes of the discipline that most Celtic patterns are on a square or rectangular grid and generally are faithful to the setting-out. But the Celtic artist could and did ignore the discipline at will yet still build on the underlying skeleton of the art.

At the small scale of the manuscripts, even a quill stroke covered a significant part of the pattern space, yet every shape, in both single- and double-interlacing, was carefully outlined before filling in with colour. Some wandering was inevitable, so that now it is difficult to distinguish between deliberate and accidental departures from the assumed setting-out lines.

The *Lindisfarne* folio 12 pattern is an example which gives little opportunity for departure:

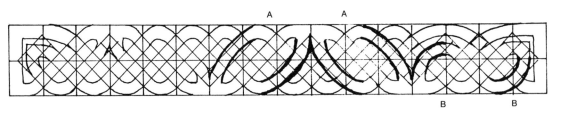

Sometimes there is rounding-off, as at A or B, with the tighter curves at B the more likely to have been sweetened deliberately.

The sweetening of curves can come naturally in the finishing process. The following pattern is repeated five times on *Lindisfarne* folio 11:

Cord thickness adjustments in single-interlacing
Cord thickness can vary from thin lines to pattern-filling knots, but
within any pattern the aim should be for constant cord thickness
unless variable thickness is specifically intended or chosen.

Constant thickness adjustment
Although the underlying construction is the same, cord thickness
varies within manuscripts and on the stone carvings. Generally,
however, the *Lindisfarne Gospels* follows the Grid Cell, the
diagonal cord thickness (n) and the space between being the same,
whereas in the *Book of Kells* the cords are often thinner, and in the
Book of Durrow and the stone carvings they are often thicker.

Making the cords thinner or thicker affects the minimum pattern
space:

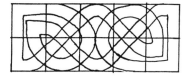
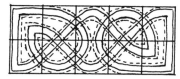
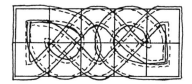

Even at this comparatively large scale the effect of drawing quite
thin lines slightly inside or outside the setting-out lines is dramatic.

Running the thick cords outside the pattern space solves nothing
because the cords overlap internally, but the pattern space need
not be reduced for the thinner cords since the extra background
balances the design:

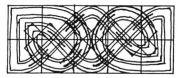

Here all short curves are set out. Round
off as desired.

Reduce the cord thickness and mark the
interlacing.

finish off.

With wide cords it is necessary to flatten the curves:

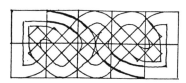

Here two long curves can be used to aid the flattening which does
its own rounding off. To guide the finishing treatment, sketch in the
shapes until satisfied. You can see that not much thickening is
needed to fill the pattern space.

Chapter 9

The Wide-cord Cell and *Lindisfarne* double-interlacing

The widest constant cord width occurs when two pairs of curves meet in a corner and 2t = u.

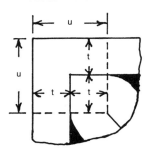

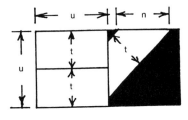

n = 1.414t, and since 2t = u, n = 0.707u, which in fractions is either $\frac{2}{3}$ or $\frac{3}{4}$u.

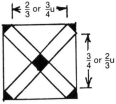

The Wide-cord Cell.

This makes tangible the approximate geometry of the Wide-cord Cell, thus providing another way of constructing wide-cord patterns. If working by measurement, use whichever fraction suits your scale.

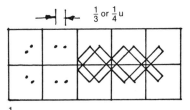

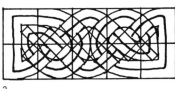

1

2

3

1 Mark the mid-grid third- or quarter-points and draw the diagonals, which meet the grid lines at the sixth or eighth points.
2 Sweep in the curves, with the grid and mid-grid lines as controls. Mark the interlacing. With thick cords it helps to interlace a centre-line throughout the pattern.
3 Finish off.

The 3:4:5 grid at the flatter end of the Celtic scale:

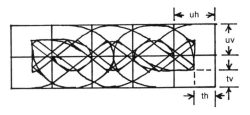

A. Unadjusted

B. Adjusted

Above left th is wider than tv, so that adjustment is needed to obtain constant cord thickness. But there is a choice, and you may prefer A to B.

The approximate geometry which produces such easy flowing
curves for the outer and inner cord lines is illustrated by the sketch
below. This shows the relationship between the square grid, the
'long curve' circles and the eccentrically placed 'short curve'
circles.

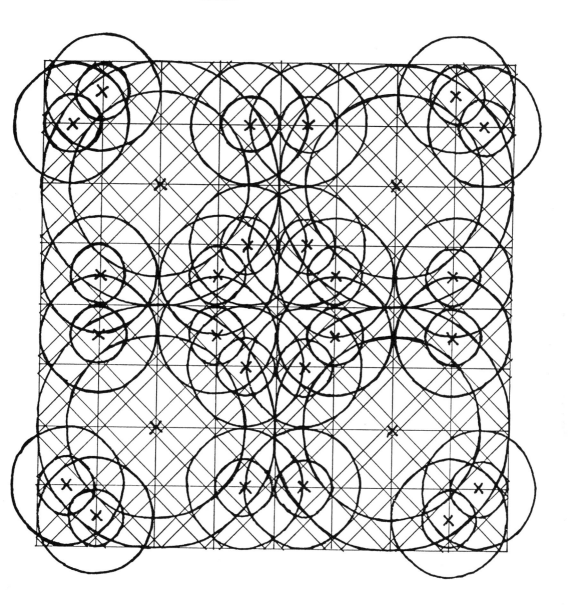

The geometry is approximate because the theoretical diagonals fit
neither circle, hence there need be no hard-and-fast rule about the
diagonal spacing ($\frac{1}{3}$ or $\frac{1}{4}$u). In the above sketch, u is 16mm and the
diagonal spacing is 5mm, or nominally $\frac{1}{3}$. This suits the large circle,
but makes the small circle slightly boxy, although not noticeably so
even at the large scale.

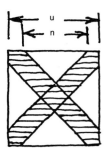

If the grid-units are neither square nor rectangular, the uneven spacing of the diagonals in the Wide-cord Cell requires care. It helps to visualize the cell as a narrow diagonal cross.

A 4u × 6u panel:

1

2

1 Guess the third- or quarter-points all round the margin, and from them draw nominally parallel diagonals straddling the grid crossings.
2 Draw the curves and finish off. The smallest grid-units fix the cord thickness.

If constant cord thickness is not paramount, the space between the diagonal cords can be reduced until it is represented by a single line. This leads to an interesting n = u construction, which is described in Chapter 11 on pages 96 and 97.

Lindisfarne double-interlacing

Double-interlacing is much more common in the manuscripts than on the stone carvings. Generally thin cords occupy what would be the edge lines of single-interlaced cords, with no adjustment needing to be made to the positions of the Grid Cell setting-out lines.

In the *Lindisfarne Gospels*, however, most of the knotwork is double-interlaced, and in these patterns a relatively thick cord was used, roughly the same thickness as the spaces between the diagonal cords.

The Grid Cell setting-out may be used. This pattern is from *Lindisfarne* folio 95 (Plate 2):

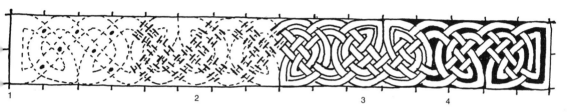

1 Spot the crossing centres on the setting-out diagram.
2 Mark the interlacing by spacing the cords at each junction.
3 Link the cords.
4 Fill in the background.

But the Wide-cord Cell is more precise:

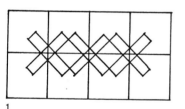

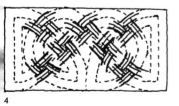

1 Draw the grid and diagonals. The third points are used here.
2 The final setting-out – draw the curves and add a centre-line. Centre spot the crossings.
3 Start the finishing treatment – space the cords around the centre spots, establishing the interlacing.
4 Emphasize the interlacing among the many pencil lines.
5 Link up the cords.
6 Fill in the background.

You may feel that tedious work is involved. The scribes drew their patterns to a much smaller scale and used very fine lines for the cord edges before filling the cords and the background with colour.

Some *Lindisfarne* designs:

Folio 95 (Plate 2)

The ratio of the grid sides is approximately 4:5, with a slope angle of about 39 degrees.

Folio 27 (also folios 2b and 94b (Plate 1)): square grid.

Curves may be sweetened if desired, but there is less need than on single-interlacing.

Folio 95 (also single-interlaced on folio 211): 3:4 grid.

Folio 27: square grid.

The original meticulous drawing is shorter in length than the width of this poor effort. The diagonals are spaced by eye.

Plate 5. Folio 124V from the *Book of Durrow*

Plate 6. Folio 125V from the *Book of Durrow*

Chapter 10
Filling a panel
including some
reconstructions

A simple arrangement of square grid-units, from the *Lindisfarne Gospels*, folio 11.

1 Mark the quarter-points around the margin.
2 Draw the diagonals.
3 The setting-out.
4 The finished pattern, handed.

Try other patterns – there are many.

A rectangle

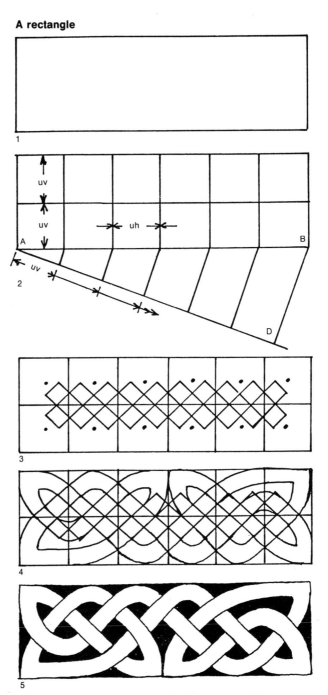

1 This panel is closely similar in proportion to one on *Lindisfarne* folio 211.
2 Make it 2u wide and measure the horizontal value as shown.
3 Locate the grid centres or spot these by eye. Follow with the quarter-points and draw the diagonals. As a check, grid and diagonal crossing points should coincide.
4 The setting-out diagram.
5 The original finishing treatment is double-interlaced.

But what if a more complex pattern is desired?

Divide the 25 × 80mm panel vertically into 3 or more units. With 3 units, either 10, 9, 8 or 7 horizontal units can be used.

Division can be done graphically or by measurement. A pocket calculator quickly reels off awkward multiples.

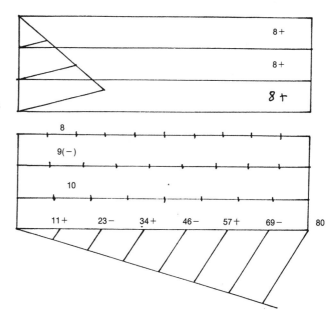

These patterns are developed from the motifs on page 61.

The diagonal angle in A is slightly steeper than 45° and in D is slightly flatter than 37° but neither is noticeably so (they are 46° and 36° respectively).

$$\frac{25}{3} = 8.33\text{mm} = uv = uh \text{ (square grid).}$$

$$\frac{8.33 \times 4}{3} = 11.11\text{mm} = uh \text{ (3:4 grid).}$$

$$\frac{80}{8.33} = 9.60 \text{ or to the nearest whole number 10 units max.}$$

$$\frac{80}{11.11} = 7.20, \text{ or to the nearest whole number 7 units min.}$$

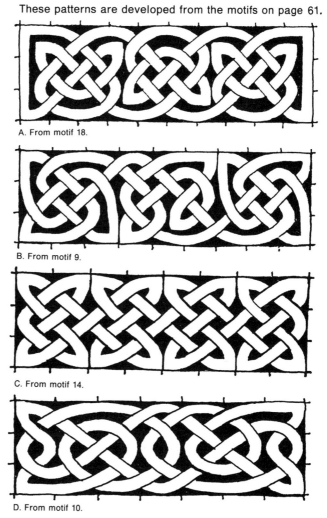

A. From motif 18.

B. From motif 9.

C. From motif 14.

D. From motif 10.

An irregular shape
A detail from the letter Q on *Lindisfarne* folio 139. The original interlacing is part double and part wide-cord.

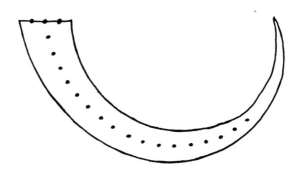

The horn base is divided into 4 units, and there are 17 larger units (roughly 5:4) along the centre-line. Where these end the horn is less than a unit wide.

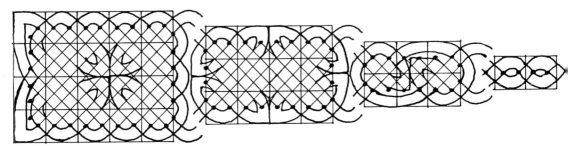

The grid reduces in stages to one unit wide. In each pattern, return loops are formed, so that only the outer cords continue from stage to stage.

In the final tapered setting-out, the loose ends link up. The whole is drawn freehand, including marking the quarter-points. There is some adjustment for constant cord thickness in the finishing.

An annular (ring) panel
This example is on the monumental cross at Lastingham, Yorks (page 11). The basic pattern is Romilly Allen's Knot 4.

1 Draw the ring to these proportions, 2 units wide. With the outer radius mark off 12 units around the circumference.
2 Add margin circles if desired. By eye, mark the quarter-points around the outer margin. Lining through the centre, mark the quarter-points on the other grid and margin circles. It helps to mark the quarter-points on the radial grid lines also.
3 Draw the 'diagonals' and form the plait. You will soon get the feel of the curved 'diagonals'.
4 Break 'horizontally' where spotted on figure 3.
5 Break 'vertically' where spotted on figure 4. Mark the interlacing.
6 Apply the finishing treatment. The 'pointed spades' are blunt.

You will find that the varying cord thickness will disappear as you proceed onwards from stage 2.

A full circle panel

A 'budding' version of the Hilton of Cadbol 'flower' (opposite).

The basic 5-cord (2½u) pattern. The circle below is 3½u radius.

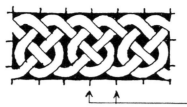

The mid-grid curves peak at the vertical grid lines.

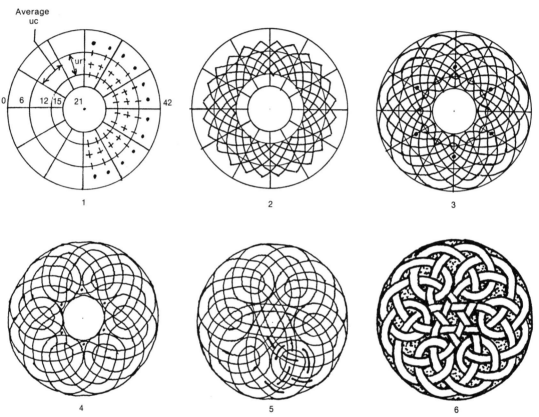

1 The 12u circular grid and quarter-points: u radial is 6mm. It is desirable for u radial and the average value of u circumferential to be roughly equal.
2 The diagonals, meeting the grid lines at quarter-points.
3 The plait.
4 Break where spotted on figure 3. You will find that some smoothing adjustment is needed.
5 Break where spotted on figure 4, and weave the cords through the centre. Mark the interlacing.
6 Finish off.

(In figures 4 and 5 the grid lines have been omitted for clarity.)

The circular pattern on the Hilton of Cadbol stone, Ross-shire (frontispiece).

Left is a rectangular representation of the pattern. 12 outer loops reduce to 6 inner loops, which disappear leaving the diagonal cords to pass through the centre. The pattern width, corresponding to the circle radius, is $5\frac{1}{2}u$, and u radial is 7mm in this reconstruction.

Imagine the helpful grid line quarter-points in the first quadrant. These have been omitted for clarity. Averaging the setting-out lines should produce constant cord thickness. The variations you see are drafting ones.

This pattern is an excellent example of creative freehand geometry. The cord path is continuous.

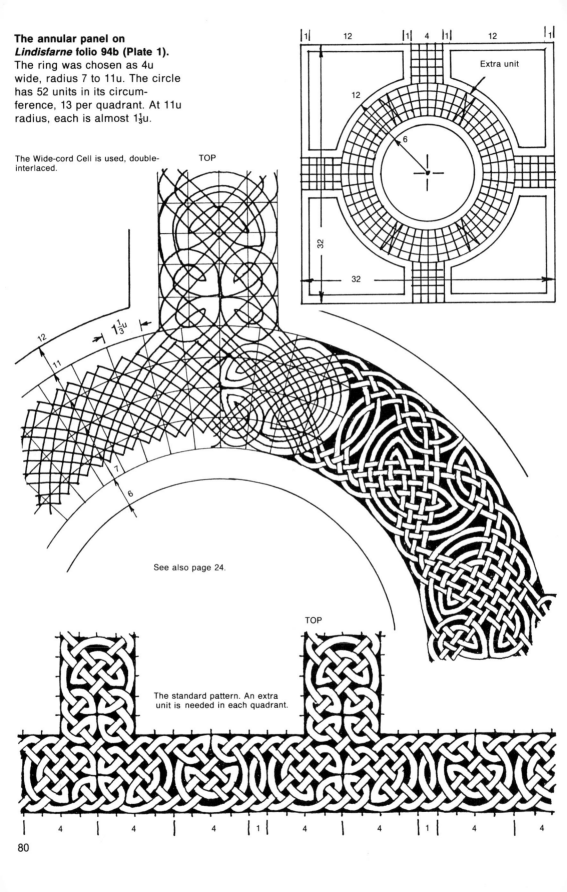

The annular panel on
***Lindisfarne* folio 94b (Plate 1).**
The ring was chosen as 4u
wide, radius 7 to 11u. The circle
has 52 units in its circumference, 13 per quadrant. At 11u
radius, each is almost 1⅓u.

The Wide-cord Cell is used, double-
interlaced.

Extra unit

TOP

See also page 24.

TOP

The standard pattern. An extra
unit is needed in each quadrant.

The centre panel on *Kells* folio 290V (Plate 8).
This is a straightforward Grid Cell construction. The pattern repeats every 3 units and an extra unit is used on each side. The rhomboidal grid gives the setting-out diagram 2 cord thicknesses, the thinner being preferred in finishing.

The corner treatment varies. The bottom corner is defaced and the treatment here is suggested, as is the colouring which is stained and defaced in places.

top

Colour key:

White

Yellow

Red

81

Durrow folio 125V (Plate 6): the border pattern in standard form. Only short and long curves are used, except for lane changes in the corners. Normally opposite corners are identical, but here the top right and bottom left corners are treated differently. A reconstruction is opposite.

Durrow folio 125V (Plate 6): a reconstruction of the border pattern.
The grid ratios are approximately as shown here, square for the 4u pattern and 4:5 for the 3u pattern. The Wide-cord Cell is used.

The cord colours:

Yellow

Green

Russet

The background crosses are not emphasized. The block colouring is typical of much knotwork, particularly in the *Lindisfarne Gospels*. The speckled cords are blue and the others red.

The four crosses on *Kells* folio 291V (Plate 3).

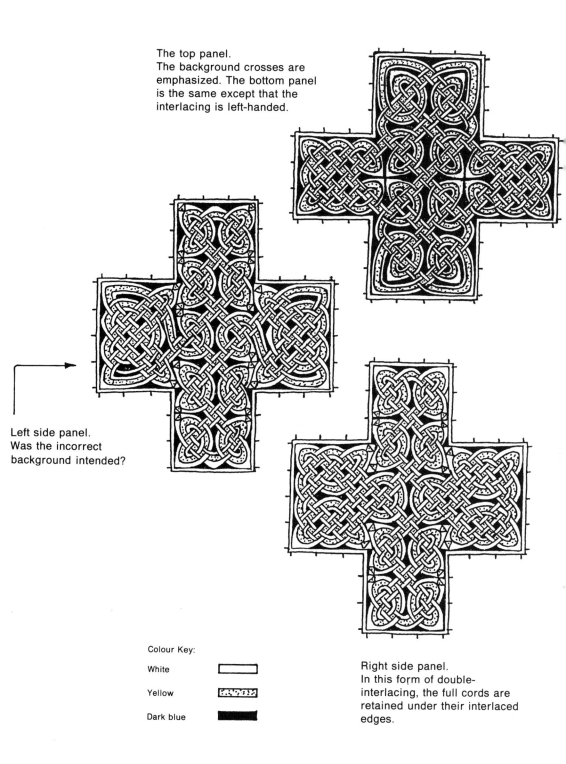

The top panel.
The background crosses are
emphasized. The bottom panel
is the same except that the
interlacing is left-handed.

Left side panel.
Was the incorrect
background intended?

Colour Key:

White

Yellow

Dark blue

Right side panel.
In this form of double-
interlacing, the full cords are
retained under their interlaced
edges.

Triangular knotwork

Triangular knotwork (which is commonest on stone carvings in Eastern Scotland) is made possible by introducing diagonal cuts to a plait cut-out. Here is the evolution of the simplest triangular panel:

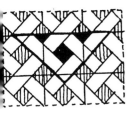
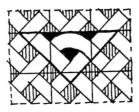
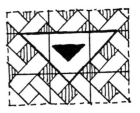

Because the triangular construction allows the cords to tuck into the corners without being trapped, the above quarter-point grid setting-out is unnecessary and can be simplified.

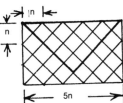
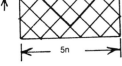

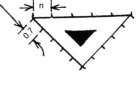
0.707n (But say ¾n)

The marginal cord approximately bisects the diagonals (the t = ¾n rule).

The 5n panel:

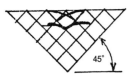

The 6n 45° panel:

In these triangular patterns, just sweep and balance the curves.

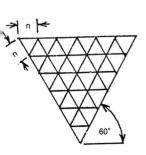
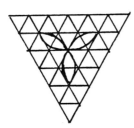
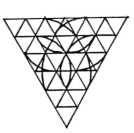

The 6n equilateral panel:
The Triquetra.

Add the third diagonals, and draw the inner lines of the curves first, starting from the centre. A good example of this symbol is on monument No 2 at Aberlemno, Tayside: can you spot it on page 2?

There are few examples of triangular panels on their own, but
many patterns become possible when triangles are linked to each
other.

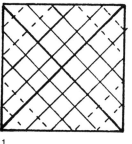 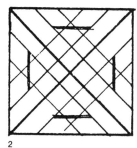 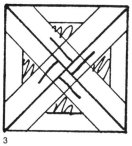 

1   2   3   4

The 5n 45° triangle:

1 The first two diagonals in from the corners are never required.
2 Draw the marginal cord edge, bisecting the diagonals.
3 Mark the interlacing and the background.
4 Finish off. A swastika's arms turn anti-clockwise from the centre.
  These often turn clockwise so that any significance is not readily
  apparent.

5 The continuous version is on the Maiden Stone in Aberdeenshire.

A 7n variation, with its continuous version below. A single example
is on stone No 5 in the Meigle, Tayside, museum and a continuous
version is on the Maiden Stone in Aberdeenshire.

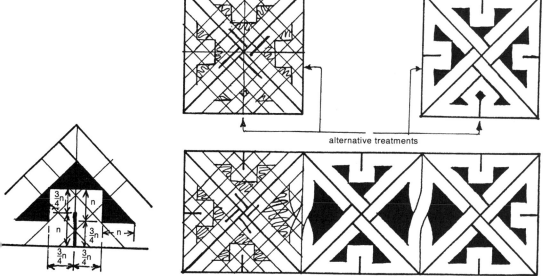

alternative treatments

6n The Stafford knot.

A variation from the
Ulbster Stone, Caithness.

6n

6n

Many triangular patterns can be constructed with a choice of n numbers. On stonework the minimum practical n number was often used, producing tight knots. The 5n plain triangle on the previous page looks well proportioned in the continuous version, but could be tightened into a 4n version or stretched to 6n or more. Because of this, and because of varying finishing treatments, the following suggested reconstructions apply to the example named and need not apply to other surviving examples.

7n – this version seems to fit another Meigle pattern, Stone No 27, Meigle, Tayside. The centre-line is incised.

An overtight 4u version of this appears on the stone cross at Penmon, Anglesey.

The 'Viking' construction on pages 96 and 97 suggests itself, and confusion is reduced if double diagonals, more closely spaced than in the Wide-cord Cell, are used.

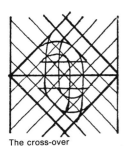

The cross-over

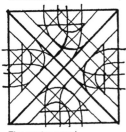

The centre panel

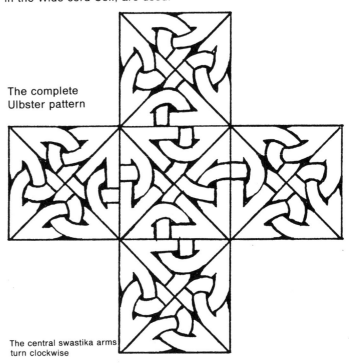

The complete
Ulbster pattern

The central swastika arms
turn clockwise

Plate 7. Folio 191V from the *Book of Durrow*

Plate 8. Folio 290V from the *Book of Kells*

Triangular knotwork was used frequently on stone carvings but rarely in the manuscripts. An exception is this version of the simple 6n Ulbster knot on *Lindisfarne* folio 139. The 'diagonals' are horizontal and vertical:

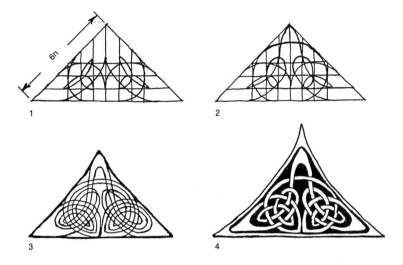

1   1 The basic pattern.
2   2 Cross over the cord lines as shown.
3   3 Slightly curve the pattern sides. Trisect the cords.
4   4 The finished design. The interlacing is the same at every double crossing.

Another Ulbster pattern.

To use a motoring phrase, these triangular panels have no strict lane discipline. Triangles are butted together with little or no space between the diagonal cords, and, as shown above, the same can occur internally.

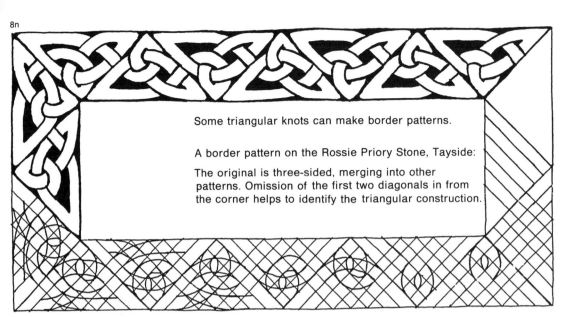

Some triangular knots can make border patterns.

A border pattern on the Rossie Priory Stone, Tayside:

The original is three-sided, merging into other patterns. Omission of the first two diagonals in from the corner helps to identify the triangular construction.

The corner treatment shown above forms a square version:

The triangle need not be right-angled. This pattern on the Eassie Stone, Tayside, uses 3:4:5 triangles.

This extends into another pattern where indicated, and could in fact be extended in all directions for an overall pattern.

This pattern at Dunfallandy, Tayside is identical in setting-out to the Eassie pattern opposite except for the curves replacing right-angled bends.

This also makes an overall pattern. On the stone, the double pattern is repeated downwards more than once, but the finishing-off is indistinct.

The Aberlemno Stone No 2, Tayside (page 2), uses the Eassie pattern in the side triangles, but 14n wide instead of 13n. The panel proportions are 14 and 12, vertically and horizontally.

Quadrantal knotwork

This is a natural development of triangular knotwork.

1

2

1 The smallest triangular panel: the 4n plain triangle.
2 Convert to a quadrant with a marginal cord, of thickness t by construction. You might find t useful as the scale unit for these patterns.

This inflated version of the triangle will accept 4n(t) versions of the Stafford and Triquetra knots. There is a similar arrangement at Penmon, Anglesey, where single Triquetra knots fill the spaces between the arms of the cross.

Try 5n versions of these to decide which you prefer.

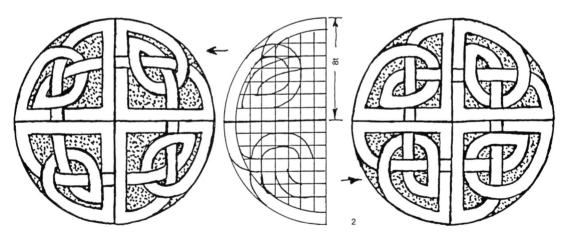

2

A pattern on the back of St Vigeans Stone No 1, Tayside.

1 The approximate proportions of the carving.
2 The straightforward or basic rendering.

If this was the construction-method, was the actual rendering a deliberate choice to add interest to the design?

The tendency with these quadrants was to break up the straight cords on the sides, to emphasize the circular appearance of the whole pattern, as in the Triquetra above and in the patterns which follow.

Suggested by the Aberlemno
Stone No 2, Tayside:

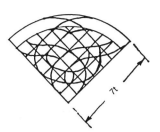

Patterns from the Aberlemno
Stone (page 2):

There are three circles on the
stone, contained within tapered
sides. The large scale which is
here used for clarity only allows
room for two on the page.

The construction applies to
circles 1 and 2, which are
identical except for the cross-
over spotted in circle 2. In circle
3, which is not shown, the side
quadrants are different again.

This design is a good example
of controlled freehand work. The
quadrant radius is 10t, making
the pattern width 20t.

The strange *Book of Durrow* — folio 21V: the basic pattern.

There is no grid. n equals u, and the diagonals run into the corners as in triangular knotwork. The pattern repeat is 5n with an extra unit on each side to enable the corners to be turned. A reconstruction is opposite.

This form of construction seems to be a link between triangular knotwork and the n = u construction described on pages 96 and 97.

Durrow folio 21V (Plate 4): a reconstruction

The diagonal slopes are approximately as drawn here, 37° and 45°.

The cord colours:

Yellow

Russet

Black

An interesting tight n = u knotwork construction, if constant cord thickness is not paramount:

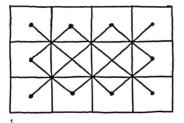 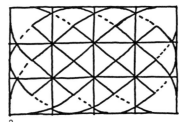 

1   2   3

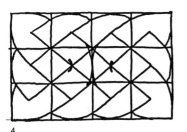  

4   5   6

1 Mark the grid centres round the margin and draw the diagonals.
2 Link the diagonals with smooth curves. The dotted lines provide a clue to the interlacing.
3 Draw the cord edges *inside* the setting-out lines. This completes the plait.
4 Make a break to form knotwork.
5 A centre-line aids the recognition of the cord edge lines.
6 Finish off, working inside the cord lines.

This variation of the Wide-cord Cell has the appearance of rush or willow weaving, and must have been common knowledge. Similar patterns are tooled on leather shoe-uppers in the Viking Centre in York.

Here are three of many possible arrangements:

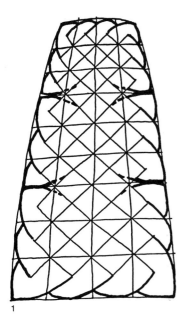

1

2

1 The spacing of the horizontal grid lines is graduated.
2 The same arrangement, with different breaks.

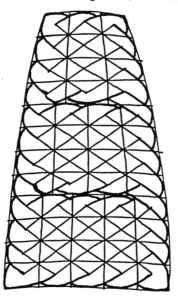

Here the number of grid-units is graduated.

There is a primitive squareness and tightness to these patterns which is absent from the manuscripts and most of the stones, except for a few triangular knotwork carvings. Are these features of Viking origin?

Durrow folio 191V (Plate 7): how the simple 2u plait produces this border pattern.

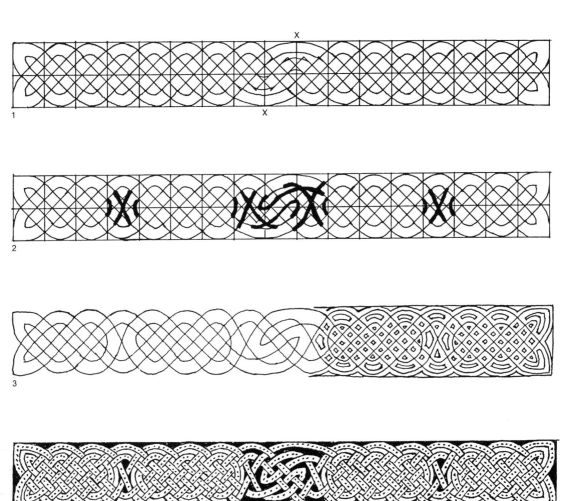

1 Draw the basic plait with horizontal breaks at X.
2 Treat each line as a cord, and break and rejoin as shown.
3 Double-interlace the Grid Cell setting-out as shown on page 71 or
   proceed as described by George Bain, by establishing the
   background spaces. This widens the pattern.
4 The finished border pattern.
   The background is black and yellow. The cords have a dotted
   centre-line.

An intriguing centre-line construction-method

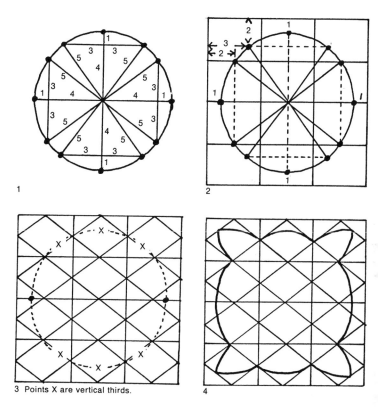

1

2

3 Points X are vertical thirds.

4

1 How the 3:4:5 triangle assists the freehand drawing of a circle.
2 The circle situated in a 3:4 grid.
3 The circle in relation to centre-line Grid Cells.
4 The approximate geometry, guessing the grid *quarter*-points.

Develop into the Woodwray pattern shown on pages 18 and 110:
Try completing this alternative end treatment!

Putting half-circles back to back produces the pattern on a stone at Norham, Northumberland (page 52). In this pattern the centre-line remains, being incised on the stone:

If the Centre-line Cell can be used with the 3:4 grid for pattern construction, can it also be used with a square or any other grid? Certainly it *can*, but has it any advantage over the Grid Cell or the Wide-cord Cell? Compare the setting-out diagrams:

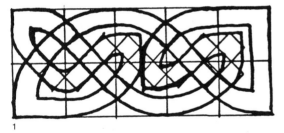
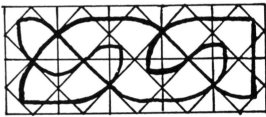

1 Grid Cell setting-out diagram.
2 Centre-line cell setting-out diagram.

The great advantage of the Grid Cell setting-out diagram is that it produces a complete geometric pattern which is acceptable for finishing treatment even without adjustment. So also does a Wide-cord Cell diagram. The Centre-line Cell diagram, on the other hand, has flattened 'long' curves to be adjusted, and cord edge lines yet to be drawn.

But since there is a grid, this can be used to mark off the cord edge lines, thus making the centre-line unnecessary. If a centre-line should be required for any reason, it is easier to draw this between two edge lines than to draw an edge line on each side of a centre-line.

It would seem, therefore, that the Centre-line Cell has no advantages over the other two cells for general use.

Chapter 12
Standard pattern reconstructions

The following patterns are presented in the belief that most Celtic patterns were created in standard form before being given their final locations and renderings. They normally use the Grid Cell in a square grid with single interlacing, but an exception on page 110 requires a 3:4 grid. Often the only thing these patterns have in common with the original works is their knotwork. Suggested actual reconstructions appear in Chapters 10 and 11, and elsewhere in the book.

Some of these patterns are complete and others are not, merely giving an indication of the knotwork contained in the original versions. In producing them, however, various corner and end treatments are shown, since the construction of these can more easily be understood by observation and by practice.

Lindisfarne

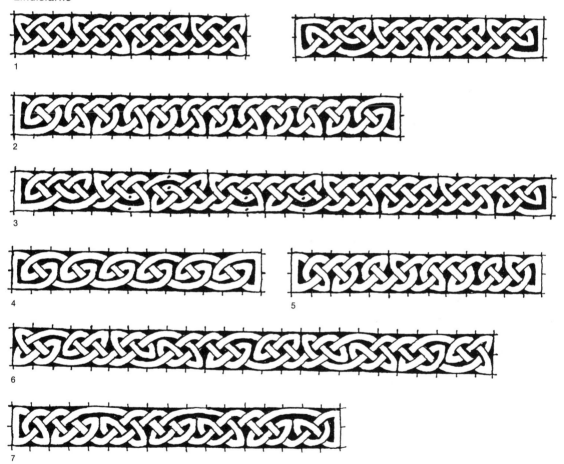

1 The folio 12 theme with different end treatments.
2 Folio 12, the semi-circular arch: compare with folio 95 below.
3 The folio 12 theme, with some extra horizontal breaks where spotted.
4 Complete from folio 95 (Plate 2). This is the folio 12 theme with extra vertical breaks.
5 Popular in *Lindisfarne*, both single- and double-interlaced. Also on *Kells* folios 3R, 124R, and *St Chad Gospels*, p.221.
6 The folio 11b theme.
7 Folio 11b: the semi-circular arch.

Lindisfarne: these three complete from folio 95 (Plate 2).

Kells folio 4V.

TOP

Column

Kells folio 5R.

TOP

Column

Kells, both from folio 3R.

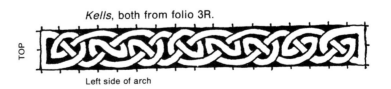

TOP

Left side of arch

BASE

Right hand column

All these from *Kells*, folio 124R.

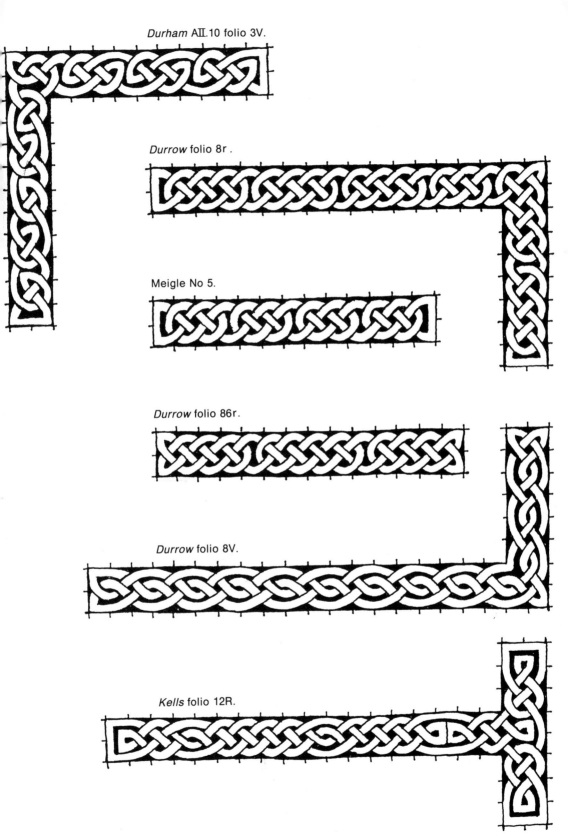

Durham AII.10 folio 3V.

Durrow folio 8r .

Meigle No 5.

Durrow folio 86r .

Durrow folio 8V.

Kells folio 12R.

Durrow folio 1V.

Lindisfarne folios 27, 29, 95 (Plate 2), 139, 210b.

Were the background crosses significant?
See also page 85.

A 4u end closure
on *Lindisfarne* folio 210b.

Lindisfarne folio 210b.

Kells folio 129V,
with different
end treatment.

Lindisfarne folios 27, 95 (Plate 2), 211.

folio 211 corner.

folio 27 corner.

Upright Knot 6

Right side

Left side

TOP

Kells folio 202V.

The right-hand border has 28 units with the internal cross appearing six times. The left-hand border has 30 units but some of the horizontal breaks required for the crosses are omitted, repeating instead the upright Knot 6.

Kells folio 2V: the cross theme again, showing corner treatment. There is inconsistency in the spacing of the internal crosses.

Other *Kells* folios containing this popular theme include folios 129V and 290V (Plate 8).

Kells folio 114V: a charming development of the pattern on *Lindisfarne* folio 12 (Knot 9).

Kells folio 114V: the second row of patterns contains motif 14 on page 61.

Each pattern lacks continuity of path, as illustrated. Was this deliberate, especially the loop below right? The continuity can easily be corrected, but the scribe's rendering is well balanced and in keeping with the overall page design. For example the end at X is curved to link up with a lion's head.

A carved stone from Monifieth, Tayside (see also page 53 and picture on page 52) – the larger scale is to show the long-curve-over-long-curve construction.

The doubled Stafford knot on the Maiden Stone, Aberdeenshire.

An unusual version of the above, linked only at the ends, on a Govan, Glasgow stone. The mason ignored the interlacing rules, as illustrated by the actual end treatment on the right. Was this intended?

The basic *Kells* folio 290V (Plate 8) pattern, with alternative end treatments (see page 81 for corner treatments): widening the doubled Stafford knot to 4u solves the linkage problem of the previous Govan pattern.

Variations on the same theme from *Lindisfarne* folio 27.

Why no horizontal break where spotted?

Kells folio 27V. Note the breaks in continuity, shown dotted.

Stone No 1, St Vigeans, Tayside (page 15) – the side pattern. The front pattern is constructed on page 111. This is composed of two arrangements of Knot 4. See page 82 for yet another arrangement, on *Durrow* folio 125V (Plate 6).

These are all doubled 2u patterns.

The 4u Stafford theme on page 109 provides an interesting variation using the 3:4 grid, where the 3u repeating knots produce a circular pattern. This, and its end treatment, appears on the Woodwray, Tayside Stone (page 18) – note the diagonals passing through the circle centres. (The Centre-line Cell construction on page 99 will also produce this pattern.)

This leads to the square grid 4u circular patterns:

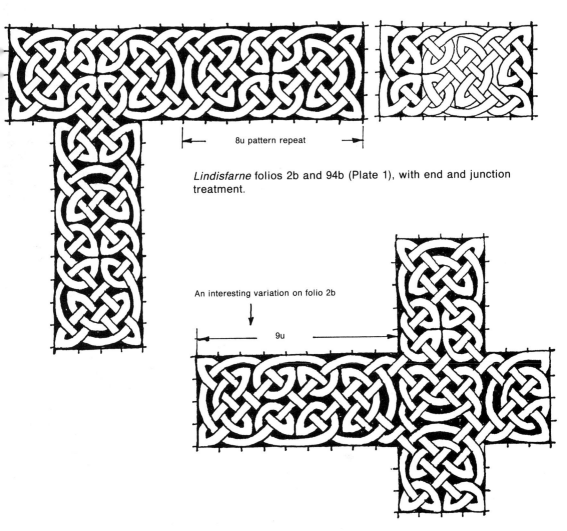

8u pattern repeat

Lindisfarne folios 2b and 94b (Plate 1), with end and junction treatment.

An interesting variation on folio 2b

↓

9u

The scribe's freehand approach enabled him to fit the 8u pattern repeat and the 9u variation into the same panel length.

An arrangement of the pattern on the Tarbat, Easter Ross stone (page 22).

Alternate circles are mirrored. The original is trebled to 12u wide, and does not strictly follow this arrangement.

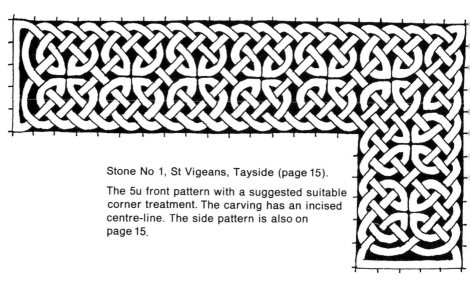

Stone No 1, St Vigeans, Tayside (page 15).

The 5u front pattern with a suggested suitable corner treatment. The carving has an incised centre-line. The side pattern is also on page 15.

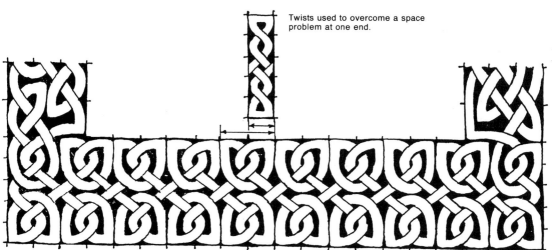

Twists used to overcome a space problem at one end.

The border end pattern on *Durrow* folio 124V (Plate 5), showing the links with the side pattern (see page 50).

These patterns suit the 3:4 grid, which has been used here, but the square grid may be used.

Suggestions for further reading and study

Until recently, few books available to the general public contained many illustrations of original works of Celtic art. The Urs Graf and the E.G. Millar facsimiles which I refer to in my Acknowledgements are not readily available except for bona fide study in some major libraries. Fully to appreciate and make use of my, or any other, construction methods, it is necessary to become familiar with the art in its original forms of application, and two well illustrated books are now easy to obtain. They are:

The Book of Kells by Peter Brown*, Thames and Hudson, 1980
The Lindisfarne Gospels by Janet Backhouse, Phaidon in association with the British Library, 1981

Sources of photographs of sculptured stones include the Royal Museum of Scotland, Queen St, Edinburgh, and the Scottish Development Department (Ancient Monuments) photographic library.

For other forms of Celtic decoration – spirals, key patterns, zoomorphics, lettering – and for my father's knotwork construction-methods, I suggest interested readers should see:

Celtic Art. The Methods of Construction by George Bain, William Mclellan (Embryo) Ltd (hardback) and Constable & Co Ltd (paperback).

* Sadly now deceased

Index